MINDFUL ANXIETY RELIEF

LEARN HOW TO MANAGE ANXIETY TO LIVE A FREE,
MINDFUL LIFE

KIMBERLY CONTRERAS

CONTENTS

INTRODUCTION

"How are you?" This is a loaded question that usually gets brushed off with a quick response of "I'm ok," and not really paying much more mind to what the person is really asking. And maybe that's the truth, that the person isn't looking for a long winded answer about how stressed and overwhelmed you are, but it is purely based on niceties and it has become a societal norm at the beginning of every general conversation. It has become an automated setting in so many of us, as has the response, that we have forgotten what it actually means. But I am here to ask, "How are you?"

I'm not asking for a fake response, a smile that barely touches your eyes, and an impression that leaves you thinking that I am such a nice and polite person. No, I am actually asking how you are. A lot of the time, when people are asked how they are actually doing, they respond with their actual pain. And recently, most people are responding with feelings of overwhelm, depression, and crippling anxiety. They are buckling under the pressure that this world has placed on their shoulders and they don't know how to fix it.

But let me let you in on a secret… I was also buckling under this intense emotional and mental pressure, and unlike a physical load, it's not something we just put down, offload, or ask someone else to help you carry. We have to find either the strength to carry this load, or we have to find a way of releasing the pressure we face. Either way, it is scary and it is hard. But all is not lost.

You have the power to change from within. I know you've heard this before, and then you've probably heard it again, and by the third time you've heard it you probably rolled your eyes and said, "not again." But just hear me out. Have you ever noticed how people who have faced terminal illnesses only really became sick and seemed to deteriorate after they heard their diagnosis from a doctor? This is because, as fascinating and powerful as our minds are, they are not always on our side. Our brain gives power to what we think is most important. So, if the brain has the power to make a terminal illness control your life, imagine what it can do if we gave positivity and our own strength that same power. We may not be able to change *the* world, but you will surely be able to change *your* world.

But change is hard to come by. As humans, it is in our nature to be habitual. We thrive off routine, and if you don't believe me, ask the mom of a toddler who just missed their afternoon nap. It actually takes us many years to grow into the adults that we are, and sometimes, even long after we have entered adulthood, we may find ourselves questioning if we're actually doing it right. Our adult personalities are a culmination of 20 or 30 years of habits and decisions which ultimately make us into the people we are. But our habits are not always the best and it takes a long time to change and fix these habits.

For example, if you find yourself growing up disliking unchangeable facets of yourself, such as the way your nose points a bit too much, or the way your ears are just too big, this is something you start telling yourself internally. You try to cover it up with your hair or with makeup, you feel overly defensive and embarrassed if others mention it, and this becomes your biggest insecurity as an adult because you made a habit of not liking this feature in your earlier years. But habits are also things as simple as smoking or even eating chocolate. The good news is that no matter how bad or stuck in these habits we are, we can change them for the better!

As we know, these habits are not always good for us, whether it is our internal narrative or yes, excessive amounts of chocolate. But what if I told you that we have the power to change these habits? Something that I have often done, and I have often found others doing as well, is make sweeping declarations about a major change that I am going to make in my life. Whether it is eating healthier, going to the gym, or even reading, I find myself setting unrealistic goals and setting myself up for failure by shouting it from the rooftops. I will tell my family that I am never going to eat chocolate ever again, or that everyday, for all of eternity, I will be going to the gym for at least an hour. And when I fail, which I inevitably do, I am met with sideways glances and comments like, "I thought you weren't going to eat chocolate ever again," as I stuff my second candy bar into my mouth.

Changing your habits are hard, but these changes can be achieved with baby steps. Start with 20 minutes a day of meditation and mindfulness and watch your entire day follow with peace and quiet. But I know what you're thinking, your day is already so jam packed with everything that is causing you to feel crippling anxiety that you can't even fathom finding 20 minutes a day to meditate. But that's alright, and it's understandable. If you can't dedicate 20 minutes to creating life-changing habits, then why not start with five minutes a day? Building a positive habit is exactly that—buildable. A small amount of time at the beginning of your day, dedicated purely to your mental space and positivity, will make your entire day better, so a little time goes a long way, and it is worth it. Eventually, doing this one small thing everyday will start to yield changes and positive results, and you will be motivated to continue. Creating good habits is not about quantity, it's about quality.

With your day jam packed and full of giving to others, you need to replenish yourself. Your overwhelm and anxiety can be eased with the most powerful weapon in your artillery—your mind. There is an old saying that says you can't pour from an empty cup, so why do we keep giving until we have nothing left within ourselves? This is where our overwhelm and our anxiety begin because we are depleting ourselves, but we are still concerned that things will fall apart if we are not giving 110%.

There is a reason why you're here reading this book. If you're facing anxiety, you feel yourself headed down the road of depression, you feel like you are constantly experiencing sensory overload, or your brain feels like it is constantly cluttered, then you may be seeking help, or advice, or you even just want to know that you are not alone and you are not the only one feeling this way.

Well, I once felt the exact same way. I faced near constant difficulties. I was always told that life is a series of highs and lows, but it seemed to me that it was just one low after the next, taking me deeper and deeper into the black hole of my life. I have sought the help of professionals but all that did was make me feel weak and unsure, and medication altered who I was as a person. But through research and undertaking mindfulness exercises, I was able to find the light at the end of the tunnel and eventually escaped. And it would be irresponsible for me not to share my experiences with you and to share what I have found to work for me. I can now live with minimal anxiety and a depression-free life thanks to applying mindfulness and harnessing this untapped power that lies within!

There are many components to mindfulness that will be looked at. It is not all about sitting in deep and quiet meditation, but sometimes, it is about journaling, meditating, taking a walk in nature, or simply just *being*. With mindful exercises, my day is focused in a positive direction from the get-go, and I am able to use certain tools to prepare myself for when I see the negative self-talk, anxiety, or stress rearing its ugly head. When you experience anxiety, especially over a long period of time, it doesn't just "go away," but you have the tools to see it coming, feel the emotions, and know how to keep it under control.

Please, don't get me wrong, this is by no means a short cut or the easy way out. Instead, it is going to take a conscious effort and it is going to require you to make consistent mindful changes, but the change you will experience is permanent, life-long, and oh so worth it!

If we don't make changes to how things are in our lives when we live with anxiety, then things won't change overall. Let us work through small changes each day, small changes using mindful tools, whether that is journaling, meditating, spending time in nature, grounding yourself physically, or simply being present when you're doing an everyday task, and watch how building these small habits can make big changes to the lives we live, which are often full of anxiety and depression. Mindfulness is not only about meditation or spirituality, it's about little tasks that can make a big difference.

Something that I have learnt during my mindfulness journey is that I can't control the world, but I can control my own response to the world. Through mindfulness, I have decided that every response will be one that I am proud of and that I am fully satisfied with.

WHY IS ANXIETY PAINFUL?

You know that feeling when you feel your body temperature rise? Your heart starts racing. You feel like no matter how hard you breathe, you can't get enough air. Your thoughts are gone but racing. You try to swallow down the lump that has formed in your throat, but it feels like trying to get down a tablet without water. You know it is anxiety. You know the feeling so well. It has been plaguing you for days, weeks, and even months on end. It feels all consuming and you try to avoid the thing that's causing you anxiety. But slowly, there seems to be more and more things that make you feel anxious. And before you know it, the only way to avoid the feeling, even for a little bit, is to keep yourself closed up in your room. And just like that, anxiety's acquaintance, depression, begins to settle in, your world has shrunk, and you feel more alone than ever before.

That's the thing about anxiety—you don't know you're suffering from it, and you don't even know that you're experiencing a full blown anxiety attack until you're in the thick of it. For the longest time, you feel like you're anxious, but you don't feel comfortable enough to share that information or those thoughts with anyone else because you're either unsure, or you don't know for certain if what you're experiencing is *actually* anxiety.

Let me help you with one aspect first: how to know if you are experiencing anxiety. Well, the symptoms are both clear and unclear. To be honest, nervousness or excitement, butterflies in your stomach, and feeling like you're about to throw up, can all be feelings of anxiety. Anxiety also feels different for so many people, and yet there are some commonalities. If you are feeling rest-less and tense, you feel like your heart may explode in your chest, your breathing is shallow and you just can't seem to get enough of that much needed oxygen in your lungs, it points to the fact that you are feeling anxiety. Some people find themselves trembling, shak-ing, shivering, and covered in sweat, while others find themselves unable to sleep, and taking their fears and frustrations out on those closest to them.

The physical manifestations are also accompanied by mental symptoms. You feel the doom and dread, and the "worse case scenario" that seems to be the only possible outcome your mind can seem to fathom. All of this is overwhelming in itself. This coupled with the existing trigger of your stress is enough to send anyone over the edge.

But, chances are, you already know that what you're experiencing is anxiety and that's the reason why you're here. I personally think that the best way to describe anxiety, with all its discomfort, is that it is painful. It is painful for more than one reason, though. It is painful because of how it feels, but it is also painful because it often feels like no one really understands. On one end of the scale, you have those closest to you telling you you need to seek professional help when your share your feelings of overwhelm and anxiety; and on the other end of the scale, you have those closest telling you that it's just in your head, that maybe you're just tired, or they're telling you to "just stop stressing." You find yourself thinking that if you could just stop stressing and being anxious, then you wouldn't have started in the first place!

This often leaves you feeling hopeless because neither answer or solution is the one you were hoping for. See, if you are anything like me, you are hoping to avoid seeking help from anyone who is going to prescribe you any form of medication. I know the strength I have, and I want to have the accomplishment of overcoming my internal challenges internally. While I do understand and appreciate the value of seeking professional help, talking to someone that understands, and gaining an insight from an objective source, I find that I have been more afraid of seeking professional help than I was to be my own source of help. And this is why:

1. Seeking professional help does provide you with expert opinions on what is chemically imbalanced inside of you. But this would mean that you would need to believe that you are facing a chemical imbalance in the first place which is causing the feelings of depression, overwhelm, and anxiety. But for me, these feelings feel more like emotions, and it feels like my mental abilities have created and given power to these specific emotions. If this is the case, it is difficult to create a correlation between an external solution (medication) to an internal problem (emotions).

2. Professionals tend to use a variety of means and ways of solving a problem, but it is often seen that these solutions are "quick fixes," or mixing and matching rehabilitation methods until you

find the one that works for you with minimal side effects. If you find yourself taking medication to ease the anxiety, it may seem like you are viewing life through a distorted lens, like you just aren't quite yourself. My own anxiety took weeks and months to form and develop into the great monster it eventually became. Anything that promised to fix my anxiety in a matter of days seemed almost too good to be true. How would I regulate myself and how would I adjust? Anxiety is not an instant response, and treating it as such is bound to cause some detrimental effects. I have kids and a family who deserve an uncompromised version of me. I can't be giving them an altered, medicated version of myself if it, in turn, is no better than an anxiety-riddled version of myself.

3. I was honestly and truly afraid of seeking professional help. Now, don't get me wrong, I wasn't afraid of seeking professional help because I was worried or concerned about the opinions of others or what stigmatizations may be associated with seeking help. We'd be naive to think these opinions don't exist, but it is not the reason I had chosen not to seek professional help. See, my reasoning is this: My body and my

mind created my anxiety as a coping mechanism. Anxiety helped me avoid everything that made me feel threatened. It was by no means an ideal coping mechanism, or even a welcomed one, but it did the trick at creating an illusion of safety, despite how entirely false that illusion was. It did become out of hand when my anxiety tried to keep me safe from daily tasks like going to the store, which ultimately led to isolation and depression. But I found myself afraid of the fact that I may be replacing one thing (anxiety) with another thing (medication) and I chose not to do so. I learned that I needed to treat the cause, not the effects.

4. The last reason why I found myself steering away from seeking professional help was that I believed in myself enough to know that I had the ability and the strength to overcome the anxiety that my own mind created. I believed in myself and I was halfway there.

There are many people who have found professional help to be the best thing that has happened for them. And I am so thrilled and happy that they found something that works for them. But it didn't work for me. And maybe not for you either, and that is why you're here. So, let us work on creating the best solutions for our anxiety from within.

UNDERSTANDING ANXIETY

The question you have in your mind is probably the same question I had in my mind when I first began my journey toward mindful living: How do I fix my anxiety from within when I don't even know where it's located? Anxiety is not physical, it's a feeling, but that doesn't mean that it is not real. I think that is where the confusion lies. It begins in our minds and in our thoughts, and these thoughts become so powerful that they begin having physical manifestations. Shortness of breath, raised blood pressure, a trembling body, excessive shaking, exhaustion, and lack of energy or motivation are all physical symptoms of this mental disease that plagues so many. I once saw an extremely profound saying stating that people always look at mental health as being somewhat "less than" when compared to physical health. When in actuality our mental health comes first. Everything we do in our lives stems from our thoughts. Thoughts become words, words become actions, actions become habits, and habits become your destiny. It is extremely difficult to have a healthy body with unhealthy thoughts. When you are feeling depressed or having anxiety, the last thing you want to do is exercise, even though in the back of your mind you know that exercise is a healthy way to release negative thoughts and energy. But you just can't bring yourself to do it. People will say that you're not depressed or you're just sad, or they will tell you to just "get over" your anxiety. But you would never tell someone that it is *just* cancer, or that they should just get over it if they are battling cancer.

The world has been wonderfully becoming more aware and sensitive to the occurrences of mental health, but they are sometimes supportive in a way that doesn't help the person who is experiencing the difficulties. So how can you, as the one who faces and lives with anxiety on a daily basis, combat this in your own life. To know how to fix something, you need to know how it works. We are going to delve into the science of anxiety.

The Anxiety Cycle

So much of life is a cycle. We have life cycles, food cycles, the cycles within ecosystems. It is understandable that there are therefore cycles within the components that make up our lives. We have hormone cycles, stress cycles, and even anxiety cycles. So, let us take a closer look at the anxiety cycle.

Our brains are extremely smart. And I know just by saying that I'm stating the obvious, but when you think about the fact that it regulates all our responses, and in particular, how we respond to situations, it is extremely phenomenal. At its most basic level, having anxiety is very much needed for basic survival. I know it seems strange, but stay with me here. There are distinguishing types of anxiety. When used in its negative form and people say that they *suffer* from anxiety, what they mean is they suffer from crippling, and sometimes debilitating, forms of anxiety and they suffer from anxiety attacks. But a healthy amount of anxiety is actually necessary for survival. You see, much like our stress response, we need a healthy amount of anxiety to keep us safe. It is what tells us to avoid dark alley ways, it is what tells us not to cycle too close to the edge of the road, and it is what tells us not to get too close to the edge of a cliff because we might fall.

Anxiety is meant to keep us safe. Just in the same way, stress allows us to maintain some sort of discipline. If we were immune to the feelings or the effects of stress, we would never be motivated to meet deadlines, and we would forget to value the little things like taking off from work a little earlier to make it on time for our child's dance recital. Stress initiates our fight or flight response, and this is directly correlated to anxiety in that the same hormones are released—cortisol and adrenaline (Schnatz, 2021). But when the threat isn't real, this is when we face unhealthy anxiety.

As smart as our brains are, it releases these same hormones and evokes the same responses from us whether we are feeling a positive or negative version of the same emotion. In simple terms, excitement and anxiety are both triggered by the same chemical reaction that is occurring in our brain. The same hormones are released when we experience excitement and anxiety (Therapy in a Nutshell, 2019). The difference however, is the stimulus towards which we are experiencing these emotions. We can have these emotions towards a positive stimulus such as a wedding or saying a speech at a birthday party. You will experience nervousness but the chances are that you are excited about it. But when the stimulus is negative, you begin experiencing anxiety towards that stimulus. For example, if you have a fear of public speaking, you won't be excited about a work presentation or even about saying a speech at a function for your loved one. This anxiety is in response to a perceived threat, something you have developed a fear towards, and it may not necessarily be a real threat. Yes, there is a major difference between something that is real and perceived.

You see, as amazing as our brains are, they have the ability to entirely construct a reality around what we fear and whether that fear is real or not. Our perception of fear is created by an experience we had with something that resulted in a negative outcome. And this is rightly so, because it helps us be more aware and more knowledgeable about things that pose a danger to us in life. Let us take an example that's as simple as cooking on a hot stove. When you learn how to cook, or even as a young child watching your parents cook, you are constantly told that the stove is hot and you should not touch it or else you will burn yourself. When you get more comfortable with using a stove, you develop a fear that is healthy enough to make sure you never place your hands directly on the stove. There is always this real and healthy fear that exists for a hot stove. But let us say, for example, you do touch a hot plate on the stove by accident. Your perceived fear of the stove may be more heightened than someone else who has never felt just how hot a stove can get. The heat and the danger that the stove gives off doesn't change, but your perception of how hot it is has changed and the danger has become greater. This may lead to you being extra cautious when you're around the stove. But this turns into unhealthy anxiety when your perceived fear towards the stove grows to an even irrational level. If you find yourself terrified of turning the stove on, avoiding cooking at all costs, and worried that any stove will almost always burn you, you are experiencing unhealthy anxiety and a negative fear towards the stove. This is ultimately what leads to the anxiety cycle.

But how does this perceived fear grow to an almost uncontrollable size? The answer is the anxiety cycle. Let us break it down and look at what the anxiety cycle is. In straightforward terms, the anxiety cycle is where, because of a perceived fear, a person avoids their trigger, which results in increased anxiety that is associated with this trigger.

- It starts with something small. The thought or the idea of doing something that makes you nervous, it makes you feel uncomfortable, and directly takes you out of your comfort zone. After all, it makes no sense to come out of your comfort zone, it's called the comfort zone for a reason, right? Let's say, for example, that you need to go to the supermarket or to the store to do some grocery shopping. But the idea of many people all crowded together in a small space is too much for your mind to handle. The social anxiety that you feel is crippling, and the mere thought of heading to the grocery store is enough to make your knees weak and your whole body break out into a sweat. You realize that more than anything, you'd prefer to do whatever it takes to stop the anxious feeling than face one more second of dealing with the discomfort.

- This leads to avoidance. Avoidance is the next step in the anxiety cycle. Something causes you to feel anxious so you avoid doing it. In an attempt to maintain your peace and your current level of comfort, you avoid going to the shopping center which is now giving you anxiety just by thinking about it. So you do the easy thing of avoiding the thing that is causing you discomfort or uneasiness. And this actually seems like a rational response at first. But the problem comes in when avoidance leads to one's detriment. This avoidance stems from an irrational fear that is essentially preventing you from doing something that has been deemed safe for many generations. This anxiety means you're running out of things to eat and you find yourself choosing hunger over food, and that is when there is a problem. There are two types of avoidance tactics that people with anxiety use and it is either physical avoidance whereby they physically avoid the thing that is causing them anxiety, or emotional avoidance, which is where they try to suppress the anxiety that they feel instead of addressing it. Let's use the store example again. Physical avoidance will be a person completely and entirely avoiding the store or supermarket because it caused them anxiety. Emotional avoidance would be them doing things that they feel may numb the emotional feeling of anxiety when they are about to face the thing that causes them anxiety. Although far fetched, this would be doing things like taking copious amounts of anxiety medication, or even trying to drink alcohol before heading out to the grocery store.

- The next step in the anxiety cycle is short term relief. You know exactly what I'm talking about. It's that big sigh of relief that comes from feeling like you just dodged a bullet or just dodged a train. But this feeling of relief may even start out a little bit smaller. It may feel like putting on comfy clothes, getting into bed, and thinking that this is what peace feels like, and that you'd choose peace over discomfort anyday. This relief is perceived as a good feeling and your mind choruses in agreement screaming that it told you so! It told you that staying home was the best decision and it was the right decision. Who cares if there is nothing to eat in the house tomorrow? The fact that you feel relief from your anxiety is more important than eating, right? This short term relief feels great but it is just that—short term. When we enjoy and bask in the relief that avoidance provides us with, our boundaries actually shrink. So when we begin thinking about doing the thing that gave us anxiety, like going to the store, our brain immediately reminds us about how good it felt to avoid the store the last time. It starts with thinking that you have to go to the store, so you get dressed, you grab your bag, and you head to the car filled with dread. Your brain panics and thinks that it has to up the stakes to prevent you from getting this close, so it floods your body with even more anxiety (or the hormones that cause anxiety). The next time you get dressed, you grab your purse, but the anxiety cripples you before you even get to your car. The time after that, you don't even bother getting dressed. Your world gets smaller, you become isolated, and this has detrimental effects on your mental health.

- This leads to the last stage of the anxiety cycle which is long-term anxiety growth. You see, the more your brain had to convince you to enjoy the short term relief provided by avoidance, the more anxiety it had to use to convince you. While the changes seem so slight because it

happens bit by bit over a long period of time,
you don't realize just how bad your anxiety has
gotten. That's the thing about facing with,
living with, and dealing with anxiety, it doesn't
happen overnight. It happens over a long
period of time, and that is actually the long
game that you engage in when going through
your healing process.

That leads us to how we address the cycle. How do you overcome this anxiety cycle and how do you get out of it? How do you get out of being stuck and buckling under this extreme and ever increasing weight of anxiety? Well, in simple terms, all you have to do is face your fears. I know that seems easier said than done, and it really is. But no one said that this would be easy, right? Facing your fears is not as easy as hopping into your car and spending long leisurely hours strolling through the aisles at the store. It's a lot scarier than just doing that because let us not forget that this perceived fear is very real to the person experiencing it. It needs to be done in a safe and controlled way that doesn't leave you facing intense anxiety attacks that leave you crippled by your fear.

How do you start? Let us consider something known as brain plasticity, or neuroplasticity. Brain plasticity refers to the brain's phenomenal skills of rewiring itself and changing its response to internal or external stimuli (Mateos-Aparicio & Rodríguez-Moreno, 2019; Banks, 2016). Brain plasticity is what allows an infant brain to grow and develop into a toddler brain, into a child brain, into a teenager brain, and into an adult brain. It has long been assumed that brain plasticity decreases with age and that, as an adult, you are unable to rewire your brain—something like "you can't teach an old dog new tricks." But this is incorrect. We have the power to completely rewire our brains entirely by altering the synapses that fire when an anxiety-inducing event occurs.

In a TEDx Talk that he presented in 2013, psychologist Dr Rick Hanson stated that you can rewire your brain for happiness. By focusing on a positive stimulus, you have a good experience, you install the experience in your mind, you absorb it, and then you use that positive experience to undo a negative one (TEDx, 2013). He states that within our brain, neurons that fire together are wired together. This allows you to overcome negative memories with positive experiences (TEDx, 2013).

If we put this into perspective, let us say that at the ripe age of 35, or 45, or even 55, you have been given the opportunity to start a new job. With this new job comes the task of learning a new skill. This can make anyone nervous, but you end up acquiring these skills and thriving at your new job. This is because, for the longest time, it was always assumed that brain plasticity ended at the age of 25 (Fishbane, 2015). But this has been proven wrong showing that well into adulthood, we have the ability to adjust our mindsets and change our thought processes. With a combination of exercise, focused attention, and keeping your brain active, you can maintain plasticity long into adulthood.

Evidence of neuroplasticity of brain plasticity has become more and more evident. In the past, it was prominently seen in even some extreme cases. In cases of extremely severe epilepsy in young children, where medication provided no relief, it was medically recommended that the kids should undergo a hemispherectomy. This procedure is extreme to say the least and it involves the removal of an entire hemisphere of the brain (Cleveland Clinic, 2020). As this procedure was generally only done in young children, the remaining hemisphere of the brain was found to take on the functions that the removed side would generally control.

For example, language is a function that is lateralized to the left side of the brain (Ries et al., 2016). This means that the left side of the brain houses most of the language control centers. This has been proven by many medical studies. However, if a child who has undergone a hemispherectomy had their left hemisphere moved, the plasticity in their right hemisphere will actually take on all the language functions that would have been controlled by the left hemisphere (Ries et al., 2016).

Brain plasticity can even be seen in more common cases of strokes and traumatic head injuries. During a stroke or a blow to the head, some neurons may die due to lack of blood flow and oxygen. Neurons are also not cells that regenerate so their death is permanent. In these cases, other parts of the brain take on the duty of the areas that have been damaged and this is evidence of plasticity (Nall, 2022).

But how do all these technical terms translate to anxiety? Well, neuroplasticity is not necessarily something physical. The neurons or parts of the brain that take on a new function are not physically growing another part that controls certain functions. It is just learning something new. So if your brain can learn new behaviors and new functions, it can also unlearn some behaviors and responses to certain stimuli. Rewiring your mind in this sense can actually allow you to approach your anxiety in a different way, and the way you would do this is by FACING YOUR FEAR.

But before you face your fear, you need to know what it is that is causing you anxiety. You need to know what your trigger is. So while your trigger may not be the store or the shopping center, it may be the fact that there are so many people around and that causes you to feel social anxiety. In your journey to rewire your brain, you may be faced with your fear in very real and terrifying situations. But the best way to face your fears and your trigger is through controlled and safe ways. So instead of just heading to the store and diving straight into the deep end, you may consider taking a drive past the store. You see, when you prove to yourself and your brain that the perceived threat that was causing your anxiety is not as great as you perceive it to be, you give yourself the opportunity to overcome that fear.

In doing so, you slowly unravel a false perception that was formed in your mind. This false perception was a fear that grew uncontrollably in your mind. Now remember, this is not going to be a stroll in the park, the fear you feel is very real and you need to slowly test your boundaries. But just remember that your mind was strong enough to create these fears, it is strong enough to overcome it. Coming out of the negative and often debilitating effects of anxiety through mindfulness is not a shortcut and is not the quick way out. But it is worth it!

2

THE MIRACLE OF MINDFULNESS

You cannot control what happens to you, but you can control your attitude toward what happens to you, and in that, you will be mastering change rather than allowing it [the change] to master you.

— BRIAN TRACY

I think we could all agree that the feeling of being out of control is quite terrifying. This is why after a night of heavy drinking, most people look back on the previous night with intense regret at the fact that they had no control over what they did and said, and it is not something they would like to relive again. It is also a big reason why seeking professional help was also a last option for me because any situation that required me to relinquish control was not one that I was going to consider, whether it was in the form of medication, or carrying out my life with my family in a different way. But we don't really think about the fact that when we have extreme forms of anxiety, our anxiety is what is controlling us.

The common thread that you are going to see throughout the book is how powerful your mind is. This is to place emphasis on the strongest tool you have that can either make or break your entire existence and perception of the world. If we can take control of our thoughts, then we can take control of our anxiety and our stress. But how do you take control of your thoughts? Through mindfulness.

When we live in a state of stress and anxiety, we live in a sense of no control (TEDx, 2017). Our minds are cluttered and even if we are present, we are never fully present. Have you noticed when you're filled with stress and anxiety, you tend to snap more, your threshold for what you can handle seems to be almost nonexistent, and your family tends to get the short end of the stick because you snap at them when they ask you to do anything that may already add to your already-overflowing stress levels. When you are stressed and when you are facing anxiety, I'm pretty sure that we can agree that you are living in a state that is below your best. You are agitated, your mind is full and cluttered, and you are filled with despair. The anxiety creeps in and you feel it physically and in your mind. You are surrounded by people, but you are isolated and alone, and you feel completely and utterly disconnected (TEDx, 2017).

When you are constantly surrounded by stress and anxiety, you create, almost unknowingly, a negative habitual state for your life (TEDx, 2017). But the thing is that stress, or the causes of stress, are ever-present in life. We have jobs that we go to, family commitments, social commitments, and avoidance in the name of self-care is already a bad sign. How do you go through life without being controlled by your stress? It's not like we can leave our stress from a day's work at the door and put on a smiley face before entering our home. The reasons why stress bothers us so much is because we either embrace the stress until it hurts us on the inside; we try to escape the stress which gives us the brief, temporary, and shallow joy (as we do with the anxiety cycle); or we replace an inconvenient truth with a convenient lie to help us cope (TEDx, 2017).

A lot of anxiety and stress is formed from worries about the past and the future. This is the inclination of many, to focus on what would have, could have, or should have happened, or worry about what might or should happen in future, so much so that we forget to focus on the now, and on the present. This anxiety and this stress about the past and present is a perfect example of something that we can't control, and is rather something that controls us. Worrying about the past or the future, or allowing a past experience to shape how we feel about something in the future, is enough to drive us insane. There is no guarantee that things will happen in the exact same way that it previously happened or the way we expect it to happen.

If you had a bad experience at a theme park where you ate way too much junk before hopping onto the roller coaster, you may feel hesitant about eating before going on the rollercoaster the next time, or you may decide to give the rollercoaster a skip altogether. But you won't allow that one experience to taint every future excursion to the theme park. You won't let that experience stand in the way of you taking your kids to experience the joy of a theme park. We can neither change what has happened in the past nor do we have any control over what will happen in the future, and yet this controls our mental space. Why? According to cofounder and vice-chairperson of White Lotus Conglomerate Preetha Ji, this obsession and focus on the past and the future stems from a self-centric form of thinking (TEDx, 2017). She states that the root of all suffering is the fact that humans are preoccupied with oneself. We have selfish ways of thinking that deters us from living present and full lives. We are so self-centered that it is not about what the past did to anyone else but *us* and it is how the future will impact *our* own wellbeing, not others.

If you really think about it long and hard, what we are anxious about only really affects us. And if it does affect someone else, we are often so predisposed with the effects it has on us that we forget the effects it has on those closest to us. These self-centered lives that we live are a false truth that we have created for us that makes us weak. Instead, we can get ourselves to a powerful inner state that can set us free—free of stress, free of anxiety, and free of depression.

The way to find this freedom is through mindfulness. The purpose for overcoming depression and anxiety is to be healed forever. No one ever hopes to overcome their anxiety and depression only to relapse again and fall back into the pit. The aim that I hope you achieve by the end of this book is having a way to overcome your anxiety and depression forever. It has often been found that treatment by professionals leads to relapse despite people staying on antidepressants and antianxiety medication. Sometimes it is found that they experience this relapse while they are still on their medication. Other times, it is found that people overcome their anxiety and depression, they feel better and they decide that their job is done and they no longer need to work towards maintaining their mental wellbeing. It is actually a continuous journey and this comes back to forming habits, small habits each day that allow you to spend some time being mindful, present, and engaging in tasks that are dedicated to your mental health.

Mindfulness is a tool that has become a way for people to not only recover from anxiety and depression, but to also stay well after your recovery. It is a way to ensure that relapse doesn't occur. But once again, for mindfulness to be effective, you need to solve the problem at the source which will mean identifying your trigger. A negative experience is usually what sets off anxiety and depression, but there are other triggering events, such as loss, whether it is of a loved one or the loss of a job, or anything else of value; life-altering illness, childhood trauma, and a number of other difficulties that we may have faced in our lives. But what happens if this trigger is something simple, common, and that we usually have to face on a daily basis? What if it's something like feeling sad, or stressed, or even an action like heading out to go shopping? Life cannot be void of these emotions, feelings, or experiences, but if you find that this is what's causing your anxiety, you need to take a mindful approach and look at these emotions and experiences from all angles.

With mindfulness allowing us to look at our experiences, and our emotions from all aspects, in a fully aware way, we are able to form a different relationship with our triggers, and in fact, we are able to rewire the associations we have in our mind. And this is how it all links together. But to combat anxiety that is triggered by something as common or simple as a negative emotion that we feel often like sadness, or if it is triggered by something as simple as going to the store, your anxiety will be easily and often triggered. And this, once again, comes back to forming habits. Practicing mindfulness everyday, even just a little each day, will help you combat the feelings of anxiety that can so easily be triggered.

BEING MINDFUL

When people hear of mindfulness, we usually think of an ancient Buddhist practice where people sit deep in meditation, quiet with their eyes closed, in the hopes of experiencing enlightenment or coming in touch with a spiritual higher power. And while this is true for the most part, there is also another component within mindfulness that isn't necessarily spiritual. Mindfulness originated more than 2,500 years ago and found its origin in ancient Buddhist practices. Monks, and other spiritual high priests, would use mindfulness as a tool to achieve a singularity with their spiritual higher power. Mindfulness and enlightenment have been used as a way to achieve wisdom, and when used within spiritual practices, it helps in achieving spiritual enlightenment.

From a spiritual perspective, you can use enlightenment and mindfulness as a way of overcoming your anxiety by immersing yourself into prayer and meditation. The act of mindfulness is about being completely focused on a certain task. In spirituality, this would be focusing on being in a space of meditation. It would be about focusing entirely on being present in your time of meditation. Now, remember that this doesn't have to be an excessive amount of time taken out of your day. You don't need to make a sweeping declaration that you will spend an hour everyday in mindful meditation. This would be unreasonable and, if you are unable to commit, you will find yourself feeling disappointed. Instead, start with five minutes a day. Starting your day in a space of not focusing on what you have to do or what you need to do, but rather on just being in the moment, is a good way of minimizing the anxiety you will feel throughout the day. You set the tone for positivity and a sense of calm for each day.

But for the not so spiritually inclined, mindfulness is often overlooked as a practice reserved for those who are spiritual. However, this is a false notion. There is a facet of mindfulness that actually takes on a cognitive approach to mindfulness. In the act of mindfulness, you allow yourself to be fully present in the moment of whatever you're doing. You allow yourself to be exactly that—mindful. Being mindful means being fully present and fully experiencing each moment of each day despite and in spite of what these moments may bring (Peterson, 2022). But a lot of people mistake this for feeling happy or positive all the time. This is both unreasonable and impossible. Rather, what mindfulness tells us is that you are going to be fully present and fully aware of where you are, what you're doing, and what you're feeling, whether those feelings are good or bad.

Let me explain this. For the longest time, I believed the saying that said "live each day as if it were your last" to quite literally mean do the things you'd do if you only had 24 hours to live. I thought this meant going bungee jumping, going skydiving, and being happy no matter what happened. But this is impossible. Instead, all that saying means is be the best possible version of yourself, even when things seem bleak and down. This means fully feeling negative emotions but responding in a way that you can look back on and be proud of. It means being with your family and loved ones fully, whether you're spending the best day of your life at a theme park, or just taking in the pure joy that your kids display when running through a sprinkler without checking your phone and responding to a text or email. Basically, living each day as if it was your last means that if you should cease to be around tomorrow, the last day you lived would be one that you were proud of.

The same goes for mindfulness. Being mindful is not actively avoiding the negativity or the anxiety, but rather it is acknowledging that it exists, and being mindful and aware of what is causing those feelings. With mindfulness, there needs to come a certain sense of responsibility. For example, if you decide to be fully mindful in the moment, it means you are focusing entirely on what it is you are doing at any given point. Having a family dinner doesn't mean that I should pull out my laptop and get to work on a project because I am neither mindful about sharing a meal with my family, nor am I mindful about my work. When you make a decision to be mindful, it comes with the responsibility of committing to it. It means going to the park with my family, watching my kids roll and tumble in the grass, and play on the swings; it means feeling the wind in my hair and the sun on my skin, smelling the hot dogs at a hot dog stand, and embracing my child that comes running to me in tears after getting hurt. It is about mentally and physically ensuring that you are fully submerged into what it is you are doing and where you are doing it. It is also about not allowing yourself to be distracted by a wandering mind. When you're at the park, your mind is not on your to-do list, you are not thinking about the endless work you have to do, or the dishes that still need to be washed, or the house that needs to be tidied.

Mindfulness is the complete opposite of anxiety. Where anxiety tells you to focus and worry about what might happen, mindfulness tells you to experience what actually happens. Anxiety keeps you trapped in your mind, cowering from fears that may never actually occur, but mindfulness helps you experience everything, even the fear of what is actually happening. Mindfulness is focusing on who you are with, where you are, what you are doing, and what you are feeling.

If you find yourself struggling to be fully mindful because your mind seems to be cluttered, and you find your thoughts constantly distracted by things that are not actively a part of the moment that you are currently in, then you need to work on decluttering your mind and emptying it out. A way that I have found to be extremely helpful is by doing a brain dump and by creating an extensive to-do list. So get your pen and paper, or find yourself a journal or diary, and get to scribbling. What I like to do is start my morning with meditation, and then I try to get everything that's in my mind onto paper. If I am thinking about an orange and two apples, then I write that down to get it out of my mind. If I am thinking about how I am going to pay some outstanding bills, as well as a parking ticket I was unlucky enough to get, I write that down. We often spend so much of our day often haunted by our to-do lists. We keep reminding ourselves to check our to-do lists or to tick something off as it is done and dusted. This still leads to dread, worry, and concern. Instead, if you find yourself constantly worried about the list, just take a step back and remind yourself that there is a list. Trust yourself to know that you won't forget your list and that you will get to it. You don't need to keep your mind full of to-dos, because once you have them written down, they will be there, each task safely waiting for you to get to it.

There are some people who thrive off of checking items off their to-do list. These are the people that get a rush of happiness and accomplishment when they tick something, big or small, off their list. If you are this type of person, I would recommend that you make your to-do list as detailed as possible. That way, you can celebrate even the small accomplishments.

Much in the same way as you would make a shopping list instead of just going into the store blind, you would need to add in-depth and detailed items to your to-do list. I find myself facing a lot of anxiety if I feel like I'm going to forget something. By writing it down, I make sure that I won't forget. By breaking things down into smaller components, I am able to minimize stress and anxiety by managing my time, making sure I don't forget anything, and completely decluttering my mind.

How to Be Mindful

We've all experienced that daily drive to or from work. The one where you get into the car, start the journey, and somehow, without even thought or realization, you arrive at your destination, but it's almost as though you don't remember anything from the drive at all. You sit in your car shocked that you are at your destination but you can't recall anything about the journey at all.

This is exactly what it is to *not* be mindful. On these particular drives, there are one of a thousand thoughts running through your mind at any given second. You may also have your favorite playlist playing in the background but your mind is keeping you preoccupied. Perhaps you're focused on what happened at the office, maybe you have a deadline that you need to work on and you're thinking about the after hours work you have to put in when you get home, or maybe you're thinking about the dishes that you left in the sink this morning, the meal that still needs to be prepared, and that you need to bath and dress your kids and get them ready for the evening. With your mind being so busy, you don't have the capacity to focus on the task at hand, and while driving does become a second nature to us, we are met with a disturbed feeling when we realize that we weren't entirely focused on the drive home.

All the thoughts that are flooding our minds are keeping us preoccupied with ourselves and we are therefore not able to be present in the moment of driving. We are literally in autopilot mode and that leaves us wondering what we may have missed out on. I often find myself wondering if I had bumped into something during that drive, did I pass a major accident that I wasn't even aware of and that I could have helped by calling an ambulance. A thousand thoughts race through my mind when I realize that my muscle memory, while really good, actually allowed me to be completely unaware of the entire drive.

Now imagine missing out on valuable moments because you're not fully aware and mindful of what is happening. Remember it's not about being present in the good moments only, but also in the bad moments. Yes, you want to be fully mindful and fully present for your child's birthday party or their first steps, but you also want to be fully mindful and experience sad moments like the funeral of a loved one.

With mindfulness giving us the opportunity to be fully aware, we are no longer captives of our own anxious thoughts. But how exactly do you practice mindfulness? It is so easy to slip back into old habits, and it is so easy to be stressed about a deadline that is waiting for you at home when you're out spending time with your kids. So how do you make sure you are mindful and that you stay mindful?

The first thing you need to do and need to know is that it is a conscious effort that takes continuous practice until it is what becomes your second nature. Once again, you need to make this your habit. The next thing you need to know is that this is not going to be your habit immediately. You are in it for the long run. We know that getting rid of anxiety isn't about instant gratification. Instead, it is about tapping into your own power, which sometimes isn't as evident to us as it is to others. This means you need to bear with yourself and be patient with yourself in getting the hang of mindfulness. It means putting in the effort and reaping the rewards forever.

But mindfulness doesn't mean just experiencing the present moment, but it also means letting go of all the emotions and feelings that come with that moment, no matter how good or bad those feelings might be.

Talking about mindfulness may seem like this difficult thing to follow, where you'd have to record rules and structures and follow them to a tee to achieve any sense of mindfulness and reduced anxiety. But that is not the case. It is actually really simple with simple techniques that you can follow to immediately ground yourself and bring yourself back to the present. Whether you find yourself losing grasp on your mindfulness, or you find yourself needing to achieve a sense of mindfulness, this is what you can do to help, and how it can work directly against anxiety:

- **Breathing**—Breathing is something that is a constant in our lives. In every moment of every day, we breathe. So what better thing is there for us to use to ground ourselves? It is constant and it is physically visible. We can see ourselves breathing and we can monitor our breathing. When you feel the anxious thoughts coming in and the feeling of anxiety welling up from the pit of your stomach, you can start focusing on your breathing. Focus on the feeling of it filling your lungs and coming out. Focus on the sound of your breathing. Focus on the feeling of the air in your nose and mouth, and maybe even stop to consider smells and tastes that the air might have. In addition to grabbing and holding your attention in the here and now, deep breathing is also known to counter and deactivate the sympathetic nervous system which is responsible for the fight or flight response and it activates the parasympathetic nervous system (Peterson, 2022). One of the signs of an anxiety attack is short, shallow, and rapid breaths. So slowing down your breathing actually makes your brain really happy and regulates the imbalanced oxygen and carbon dioxide balance that the short and shallow breaths have caused, so taking deep and slow breaths is actually like giving your brain a great big hug (Young, 2016).

- **Awareness**—We've already discussed the anxiety cycle in detail and we know all about avoidance. But in complete contrast to avoidance lies awareness. Being aware not only allows you to be fully present where you are and with what you are doing, but we cannot deny that in this world we currently live in, it provides a sense of safety as well by allowing us to be aware of where we are at all times and aware of who is around us at all times. By embracing awareness, you embrace your experiences in that current moment, a lot of which is taken in through your senses. Be aware of where you are, what surface are your feet planted on? Are you on hard ground, grass, or carpets? What are you smelling? Is there a taste of anything in your mouth? Feel your tongue move along your teeth. What do you hear? The input of your senses allows you to temporarily remove yourself from being stuck inside your mind, which is a direct way of combating anxiety (Young, 2016). It is also important to be aware of otherwise mundane tasks. Remember the drive home we spoke about? Take a moment to feel what the steering wheel feels like, the pedals under your feet, the feel of the car on a bumpy or smooth road, the sounds that you hear whether it is music coming from the radio, a podcast, or just the sound of the car moving at a high speed. Mindfulness doesn't have to happen in a moment of extreme anxiety only, and you don't need to be locked away in a room to do it either. Where you are at the moment is where it can be most useful and effective (Young, 2016).

- **Accept and let go**—When you are mindful, you are not trying to control how you feel about a specific moment, but rather you are acknowledging that this is the way you are feeling and there is probably an extremely valid reason for why you are feeling this way. It's not about ensuring that you are going to have a positive response to every occurrence but rather understanding why your response is negative and letting go of the negative response without judging yourself for it (Peterson, 2022). Don't get me wrong, being mindful and having your emotions and reactions is not an excuse to be a horrible person or to be a nasty person. You still need to be accountable for your actions and reactions. Being mindful also allows you to see others being mindful without judging them and their responses. And most importantly, it is about being gentle and patient with yourself. Remember, you may not be successful with mindfulness at the first try, your brain may be scattered and you find yourself struggling to bring your focus back to the here and now. This is just the current habits you have developed over time, you are mindfully addressing to change them. You got this!

I have said it before and I will say it again, mindfulness is not a destination, it is a journey, and it is a tool to be used in your journey of overcoming anxiety. It is not a quick fix, but when you find yourself easily focusing and overcoming an anxiety attack by yourself, you will thank yourself for sticking with it.

THE POWER LIES WITHIN YOU, MY DEAR

How often have you heard people say that they live with anxiety or that they live with depression? This is honestly something that truly and deeply breaks my heart! As someone who used to "live with anxiety," and who used to "live with depression," I can tell you now that that is no way to live at all. We are not meant to live with crippling anxiety and depression that weighs down on us so heavily that we can't seem to get out of bed. But a lot of the time, people think they do need to live with it. They power through their anxiety, they fight the depression to get out of bed each day to show up. They show up for those that need them, even though they can barely show up for themselves. But like I said, this is no way to live. Instead of living with your anxiety and depression, there are ways to overcome it. I have found a way out of my crippling anxiety and my gut wrenching depression. I know how hard it can be to see the sun on the horizon, to see the possibility of getting out of that dark space. But you can and you will overcome it!

When we are in a cycle of sadness or darkness and we have been there for a while, we are actively "exercising" our sadness cycle or muscle, so to speak. We end up making this sadness stronger and stronger because we are continuously exercising it, and before long, it has an overwhelming power over us. However, gratitude, self love, happiness, joy, intuitiveness, and listening to our divine nature also takes exercise as well. It is the same as jogging. One morning you decide to take up jogging. On that very same morning, you don't expect yourself to run the fastest mile, or even a mile at all. You're going to start with a little jog, or even a brisk walk to the corner of your street. Heck, you may just even walk around your yard. And even with this slight jogging that you're doing, you will be very uncomfortable. Your body isn't used to this so you will be tired and sore.

You keep on jogging, you stick to this exercise despite the sore muscles because you know that the sore muscles are a sign of strength and growth. If you stick with it, what do you imagine you would feel like after building your consistent routine? You would be so proud of yourself for following through, your body would feel stronger, you would have more clarity of mind, your body would feel healthier, and not to mention, all the oxygen your blood was getting daily would make you feel more alive than you have ever felt before. It takes one step, follow through and the benefits will be long lasting.

The benefits of changing your mindset are the same as sticking to your jogging routine. It may feel uncomfortable at first. The five minutes you spend meditating, journaling, and exercising might make you feel fidgety. It will feel like it's hard. But with consistency, over time, you will learn to sit in silence, your metaphorical mindful muscles will stretch like they haven't before, you will release and let go of negativity through writing, you will learn new things about yourself, you can acknowledge the past if you need to, and you can let it go to make room for what your inner voice is telling you right now. Releasing the negative energy to make room for the positive. And once you experience the positive that life has to offer, you can bet that you will never want to go back to the negativity.

We know that anxiety can stem from anywhere with no rhyme or reason. There are most times when those who suffer from anxiety will say that they know their fear is irrational but they can't seem to get past the wall that their anxiety has created from them. And those that don't suffer from anxiety can't understand how this is possible. There are many triggers that can cause someone to feel anxiety in the moment. The reality is that anxiety is something we all feel almost everyday. You know that busy intersection that you have to cross on your daily commute to work? The feeling you get as you approach it is that of dread and, yes, anxiety. But each day we experience small doses of anxiety that push us to do more and do better. This daily anxiety is triggered by things that are needed. When it becomes a chronic problem is when we need to find out what our bigger triggers are.

Chronic anxiety—the type of anxiety that makes your hands shake, your breathing shallow, that makes you want to curl up in a ball and avoid the world—can be caused by a variety of triggers. As we know, stress is a major contributor to anxiety, especially when our stress is unresolved. You see, much like anxiety, stress also occurs in cycles, and when we don't complete a stress cycle, we get stuck in the worst of it where this persistent stress ends up in us having severe anxiety (Embrace Sexual Wellness, 2020). Stress is what triggers our fight or flight response, and ultimately leads to the avoidance that we face in our anxiety response.

Another cause of anxiety is that it could be genetic (Holly J., 2022). We get our eyes from our parents, smiles that we share with our siblings, quirky features that we happily point out is something we got from our grandmother, but we also get the not so great stuff from them, like cholesterol or diabetes. But what has often been overlooked is mental traits that can be genetic. Let us look at the concept of intelligence and academic performance. Researchers have found that intelligence and a person's intelligence quotient (IQ) are directly linked to the genetics that an individual possesses (Williams, 2014). We know that intelligence consists of a unique blend of innate and environmental factors, but the innate traits will even go so far as to determine the drive and ambitions that a person has (MedlinePlus, 2020).

So while triggers can be caused by an external stimulus, we can't count out the fact of genetics as a contributing factor. While it is not the only determining factor in whether or not people will suffer from anxiety and depression, we cannot entirely overlook it. In multiple studies that have been conducted on identical twins and fraternal twins, anxiety and depression was found in both identical twins who have the exact same genetic make up, showing that there is a genetic link to anxiety and depression (Benisek, 2020). But as with all other genetic illnesses and disorders, it is easy to prevent and even identify the early onset of such disorders which can allow you to mitigate, delay, or entirely remove the risk of suffering from these disorders.

If anxiety and depression runs in your family, you will likely see an early onset in those who present with anxiety and depression (Benisek, 2020). The earlier the onset, the more likely it is to be caused by genetics. Also, if you notice the signs of anxiety and depression early on and fairly consistently within a family, you will be better equipped in identifying the early symptoms and you can take proactive strategies to fight the onset (Benisek, 2020).

A major trigger for anxiety and depression is a traumatic event. The reason for this is either because we find ourselves reliving the traumatic event over and over again in our minds until it entirely consumes us, or until we find ourselves pressing it down, deeper and deeper into a black hole so that we never have to acknowledge it ever again. Pushing it down and burying it deep within means that anything that bears a slight resemblance to that traumatic event or that evokes similar emotions is going to serve as a trigger for us, meaning that we will feel anxiousness whenever faced with these emotions.

Trauma is defined as an event that causes excessive strain and stress on us, either instantaneously or for a prolonged period of time, and this stress and strain can be mental, physical, or emotional. Traumatic events can stem from anything. It could be a car accident that you were in at a young age. That car accident could have injured you slightly, or you could have lost a loved one in that accident, but still it causes physical trauma. The loss of a loved one is defined as an emotionally traumatic event. As someone who has lost many close to me, I can tell you that the simplest thought of your loved one, even a good thought, can bring you to a place of crippling depression. But burying these emotional feelings so you don't need to address them or deal with them means that you can't even show up to support your loved ones when they face the loss of a loved one.

Another traumatic event that manifests physically, mentally, and emotionally is when a miscarriage occurs. This is one of the hardest, most confusing losses a woman has to face. Not only does her body physically go through trauma by having to deliver her lost baby, but emotionally, she is heartbroken, and mentally, her mind can't comprehend what is happening. Her hormones and her mind that was just preparing to have a baby now has to undo everything and face the loss, a loss that she can see and that she can feel.

Another reason why traumatic events seem to grip some so tightly while others tend to move swiftly past it is that trauma goes by unnoticed and unspoken about a lot of the time. When people face a traumatic event, depending on what they have dealt with, they may be ashamed or even embarrassed to talk about it or admit that they need help overcoming it. Now is this the fault of the person who has faced the trauma? Not at all! Instead, it is the fault of the society that surrounds the person that has falsely led them to believe they are not allowed to address their trauma.

Although we don't have the power to control what happens around us, we do have the power to understand how to cope with our surroundings and situations by strengthening our power within. Using mindful techniques equips us to be more prepared to live through the hard times, feel the hard times, but not get stuck in the hard times. By having practices that fill and strengthen our inner selves, we will have armor to help us through the challenging times. You have the power to build resilience! You have the power to grow in hard times rather than be stuck in a cycle.

HOW TO IDENTIFY YOUR TRIGGERS

Identifying your triggers is an important part of overcoming your anxiety. It's like having a thorn in your foot. The pain and discomfort are consistent, but you have to identify and remove the thorn for the pain to ease. Now remember, we are not trying to identify the thorn so we can ignore it and hope it goes away. We are trying to identify the thorn so that we can address it and remove it.

We know that anxiety can be caused by a variety of triggers that present differently in different people. Things like having too much caffeine, eating foods that are high in sugar, some types of medications, lack of sleep, and an upcoming event that we are trying to avoid. These are the types of triggers that leave us feeling strung out and that allow external events to make us feel much more anxious. External triggers that are commonly found are financial troubles, a traumatic event, health concerns, social events, stress, and conflict.

But something we keep hearing over and over again, something that is drilled into our minds from a very young age is that we are all unique. And what triggers anxiety in you, is not going to be a trigger for me. For example, I have always been drawn to horses. These beautiful, majestic creatures seem to have the ability to see deep into the soul. Since I was young, I have had an innate and natural attraction to these phenomenal creatures. There are some people who cannot even come within 5 ft of these majestic animals because they are absolutely terrified of horses. Whether they are scared by the animal, the sheer size and magnitude of a horse, or they are afraid of riding a horse and falling off, there are some people who choose to steer entirely clear of horses. On the flip side of this same coin, I am absolutely terrified of chickens, and the mere thought of being near one sends strange shivers down my spine. So we cannot take general anxiety triggers as a rule of thumb that causes anxiety in everyone.

Instead, what you need to do, as someone who is facing anxiety on a daily basis, is identify what is *your* trigger. What sets you off? What makes your heart race? What makes your palms sweaty? What makes your knees weak? But let's be honest, you wouldn't be here, reading this book if you already knew what your trigger was. So let us take a deeper look into how you can identify your triggers.

The starting point in identifying your triggers is to first know and understand that you are not expected to go through this identifying process by yourself. No one knows you as well as you know yourself, but when you're literally the one that is in your own mind, it makes it a bit harder to be objective. The first step I can give you in identifying your triggers is to find someone that you trust and that you are willing to talk to and share your fears. Having someone to talk to is not only going to allow you to have someone with whom you can share, but when you feel anxiety so often that the anxiety attacks seem to bleed into one another and you don't know where one ends and the other starts, having an external pair of eyes can help you see from the outside what changes you go through before, during, and after an anxiety attack.

When you are the one going through anxiety, it becomes harder to differentiate between the good times and the lowest times because everything in life is tainted with the shadow of anxiety or depression. You can't see, or even differentiate between your best self and your worst self. A person that is close to you can tell you that when you start racing through your words and you seem like you're zoning out is when they realize you are about to face an anxiety attack. This can actually help you pinpoint your triggers because they can tell you that you started acting this way as soon as you saw a dog, or before you entered a room with a large crowd.

As I mentioned before, if you are hoping to seek out professional help, or you are hoping that this objective set of eyes comes from a professional, then that is fantastic. But my advice is that this is someone who is personally close to you. They have seen you at your best and at your worst, they know you with and without anxiety. A professional is someone you are going to see for two hours once a week, the person you trust is going to be someone who knows you, every part of you, even the parts you may have forgotten.

The next step is that you are going to look at whether you have an anxiety disorder or not. As we have said, anxiety is something you face everyday. But when it becomes irrational is when it becomes a disorder. This is actually one of the easiest ways of finding your triggers. By knowing what type of anxiety you have you can find your triggers more easily (Hims Editorial Team, 2021).

No one said pinpointing your triggers was going to be easy. It's going to take facing some hard emotions on your part, and it's going to take some active work. Which leads me to my next step—*put in the work*. Putting in the work stems from a place where you decide you want to get better, and that is also part of the reason why you're here reading this book. There are some who enjoy wallowing in their sadness, their depression, and their anxiety. Perhaps they thrive off the attention that they get when they face severe anxiety. But there are those who know that this is not the best version of themselves and they want to put in the work to get better.

There are going to be active and passive tasks that you need to fulfill in pinpointing your triggers. The first thing you're going to do is start recording your feelings on paper. You're going to carry a journal with you and you're not just going to write in it when you're anxious, but you're also going to write in it when you feel at peace and when you're calm and happy. This is going to allow you to look at the comparison between times of difficulties and times of happiness. You will be able to keep track of exactly what spurred on different emotions and it will narrow down possible triggers. When you get into a better flow of writing in a journal, you can then even try to find coping mechanisms that help when your anxiety is at its worst. One such coping mechanism may also be journaling itself (The Recovery Village, 2022).

Something that goes hand in hand with journaling is identifying major life events that are taking place when your anxiety is at its worst. Are you going through health challenges, are you facing the loss of a loved one, or are you in a bit of a financial bind. Knowing what your external surroundings are like at the moment of intense pressure will help you not only figure out your anxiety but associate similar events with the trigger you are feeling. This is easily kept track of when you are recording everything in your journal.

The next one is quite a difficult one, but bear with me. I never promised easy but I did promise it was worth it, right? You need to look back on past trauma, something that you know for a fact broke you. Whether it serves as a constant reminder to you or it is something you actively try to avoid, you need to come face-to-face with that trauma. Let me give you a personal example. I lost my mom, my dad, and two of my brothers in the space of five years. With each loss, I tried different ways of dealing with them. Leaning fully into the pain and emotions was too much to bear, and shoving the feelings down and trying to block the feelings out were also too much to bear. This trauma tainted everything I faced going forward in life. I lived life with constant fear because I never addressed these emotions. There was always a "what if" moment that shadowed my life. The trauma from the first loss affected how I handled each loss after that, and each one was crippling and left me broken. I went deeper and deeper into the pit of depression. Until I woke up one morning when I began my mindfulness journey and I confronted the feelings and emotions that left me cripple. You see, for as long as I avoided the trauma, the more power it held over my life. I had to face it, because we have to face loss in life. It is part of the cycle in which we live. Addressing that trauma helped me overcome the very thing that I had given power to and that began consuming me. It is also here when I realized that the pain, hurt, loss, and grief that I face are not bad emotions, but just misplaced love. When I looked at it through this lens, it took on a positive approach.

The next thing you are going to do is start listening to your body. This is something that you will start doing when you become more mindful and more present in each moment, but it takes concentration and effort. When a woman becomes pregnant, you feel the kicks of your baby as your little one grows within you. It is magical. But after you give birth, something strange happens—you feel phantom kicks. I thought this was something that went away but I realized that even after two years or four years since giving birth, I was still feeling phantom movements. Now, don't get me wrong, I wasn't going insane or anything, but when you are pregnant, your body becomes so attuned with what you are feeling that this stays with you long after you have given birth. This means that gas and normal movement in our intestines are associated with the fetal movements we were once used to. If our bodies can become so attuned to listening to itself during pregnancy, surely we can do the same thing in normal everyday life.

What you need to do is listen to how you are feeling at different times. Do you feel extra stressed out after having too much coffee? Do you notice that certain foods impact your moods in a very specific way? Do you find yourself more stressed when you are surrounded by five people than when you're around two people? Listen to your body and the feelings that you have inside. You may find yourself not only surprised that you can identify your triggers just based on the emotions you feel when you're around a certain person or at a specific place, but you will also find yourself knowing exactly when a stress response is about to occur or you're about to feel anxious because you know exactly what that feels like to you.

Easing Your Anxiety

Once you identify your triggers, you then need to find and use methods to ease the anxiety that your triggers cause. As you progress through remedying your anxiety, you will find your muscles being stronger than ever, you will have built up your endurance and you will be able to run the fastest mile that you have ever run. You will actively see the progress of starting with your running exercise. Do you just stop after two weeks of exercise and training and expect to be the fastest runner to exist? No! You keep on persisting. You don't aim to be the best, you just aim to be better than you were the day before.

Many people prefer to use natural remedies as opposed to clinical or prescription remedies. The thing about medication is that you never know what's going to happen once you stop the prescription drugs. You then have to live with a fear you once had. Dependency on any form of medication is not healthy, especially when it comes to medication used for your mind. Think about it this way: medication that is used to treat chronic illnesses like diabetes requires a life-long dependency on medication, but there are so many side effects that come with them. I faced the same fear when confronted with anxiety and depression and I found myself avoiding professional help and seeking natural alternatives instead.

From camomile and lavender, to lemon extracts and even CBD oil, there are many different natural and herbal approaches to combating anxiety and depression. The only tricky part is finding a natural supplement that you actively experience to reduce your anxiety levels. The thing about natural substances is that each person will react differently to it. So while you have some that may experience dramatic changes in their anxiety levels, there are others that report no changes at all. In some cases, when natural remedies are mixed with other ingredients, it makes it difficult to determine which specific ingredient was useful in reducing stress. And that is the greatest challenge in natural supplements.

A healthy combination of camomile tea, green tea, lavender tea, and even dark chocolate have been proven to dramatically reduce stress in many (Holly J, 2022). We also know that including lavender essential oils in a diffuser brings a calming energy into any room and makes sleep much more attainable. This is so much so that night time body lotions, for adults and babies, are infused with lavender.

Another natural supplement that has been found to be beneficial in reducing anxiety is ashwagandha. This natural supplement proves to be beneficial to assisting anxiety because it allows you to adapt to your existing conditions rather than try to avoid these conditions (Holly J, 2022). As an adaptogen, it helps promote homeostasis in your body and leads to reduced stress, anxiety, all of which are triggered by an external source. Ashwagandha not only relieves stress and anxiety, but it has also been found as a natural way of increasing energy levels and cognitive function (Holly J, 2022).

Something else that you can do to decrease anxiety if you find it recurring on a daily basis is decrease your caffeine intake. I know, we all need that caffeine boost first thing in the morning. I, for one, easily become a cranky person if I have not had my daily dose. But caffeine is directly linked to inducing anxiety. You see, the more coffee you drink, the stronger the effects of caffeine become. So if you are drinking coffee profusely throughout the day, it can quite quickly induce your anxiety. Because caffeine increases alertness by blocking the brain's production of adenosine which is what causes you to be sleepy, it increases the production of adrenaline which gives you an energy boost (Frothingham, 2019).

Now while this may be incredibly appealing to someone who hasn't had a wink of sleep at night and has a busy schedule ahead of them, someone who is already overly alert to what causes them an irrational fear may not respond very well to the effects of caffeine. Reducing caffeine, while only making a small difference, may help you on your journey to overcoming anxiety. Also, the amount of caffeine you consume will play a big role in whether or not this is actually a contributor to your anxiety. One cup of coffee a day probably won't affect your anxiety, but be mindful of everything you are consuming throughout the day. One cup of coffee may not have any effects, but if you're following that up with three energy drinks, then you definitely reconsider the caffeine you consume.

Another practice that can aid in combating anxiety is reducing your screen time. It goes without saying that the effects of social media on our generation is scary, but overall, screen time also has effects on mental health. It has been found that there is a direct link between screen time, particularly on laptops, and an increase in anxiety and depression (Khouja et al., 2019).

I think it goes without saying that exercise and physical movement does a lot for the body. Moving in space and getting your blood pumping always provides physical and mental benefits.

We have already mentioned mindfulness and mindful practices as the life blood of keeping anxiety away permanently, but if you're not a particularly spiritual person, you're probably wondering what's in it for you. On one end, mindfulness is about following a guided meditation. It takes a lot of dedication, setting time aside each day focusing on something very specific, whether it is your inner peace, your physical position, or a spiritual higher power. This is something that takes practice to achieve, especially when we're so used to the world constantly moving at a fast pace, slowing down can seem frustrating. But create and remember your end goal in meditation which would be spiritual elevation.

You can even delve deeper into spiritual practices by aligning your chakras. This can be done by lighting incense, grounding yourself with gemstones and crystals, lighting salt lamps, and reciting a mantra that works for you. If you don't know where to begin in your spiritual enlightenment journey, then guided meditation and yoga can help.

Aromatherapy and the use of essential oils can also prove to be wonderful in terms of cleansing the space that you occupy, and if you occupy a peaceful space, your anxiety will undoubtedly decrease.

Another important mindful practice is journaling. Even if you are not diving too deep on journaling, it is important to jot down important intentions. If you give everything in your day an intention, you give everything a reason, and when it has a reason, you have an argument against your anxiety that is trying to stop you from doing the task. For example, when you do your daily planning or your brain dump, you should have more or less a general idea of what needs to be done in the day and what is most and least important. If you give yourself an intention for completing a task, your anxiety can't really give you a valid reason for why you shouldn't do it.

Focus on one task at a time. Break up your overwhelming bigger tasks into many smaller tasks, and give that small task your undivided attention. Also, make contact with nature. Actually go outside, take off your shoes and make some skin contact with the grass.

It will provide you with endless benefits to literally be connected to nature.

In a TEDx talk that she did in 2017, mental health researcher at the University of Cambridge Olivia Remes provided the audience with tips to take control of their thoughts and actions to overcome anxiety (TEDx, 2017). She admitted that medication is not a long term solution because no one wants to be on medication for forever, and once you stop, your symptoms of anxiety can come flooding back. Instead, she said that you can change the way you cope with anxiety because anxiety triggers are all around us. But having coping resources is the first step in your healing journey. Here are the coping mechanisms that she provided (TEDx, 2017):

- You need to feel like you're in control of your life. How can you feel like you're in control when there are so many variables in life, at work, and at home that take things out of your control? Well, you can actively engage in activities and experiences that allow you to feel like you're in control, such as planning your meals, and sticking to time limits that you create for yourself. If you find yourself being completely and entirely indecisive about things, it can mean that you are not in control of a situation. Olivia Remes used the example of avoiding starting something because you feel like you need to perfect the skills needed to complete a task. Her advice: just do it even if you do it badly. Don't aim for perfection, instead aim to get started, and more often than not, you will realize that you "doing it badly" isn't actually bad at all (TEDx, 2017).

- Her next tip is to forgive yourself. Anxiety is deeply rooted in the past and our future becomes tainted with a bad experience we had in the past. Anxiety makes you think about what you've done wrong and it really stops us from being kind to ourselves. But if you forgive yourself, if you actually forgive yourself and stop holding your past against you, you stop focusing on what you're doing wrong and your future is no longer shadowed by the past that caused your anxiety (TEDx, 2017).

- Lastly, she says that you need to have a purpose and a meaning in life. This purpose and meaning in life usually comes from doing things with someone else in mind. Anxiety forces you to focus on yourself and yourself only. It creates a preoccupation with oneself. But the second you do something with someone else in mind, you decrease your

susceptibility for anxiety and depression
(TEDx, 2017). Whenever I do something, I try
to do it to the best of my ability with my
children and my husband in mind. This sets the
tone for eliminating my preoccupation with
myself and immediately decreases my anxiety.

There is never an excuse to live with your anxiety especially when you are trying to overcome it. You have the power to actively change your thoughts, perceptions, and your actions. The power to overcome lies within you, all it takes is some searching and some action. Never underestimate your power!

PLEASE LEAVE A QUICK REVIEW

Thank you for purchasing Mindful Anxiety Relief. Dealing with, acknowledging, and working through life's hard times. Some of that work comes from reading books to help us remember we have the power in ourselves if we take the time to learn and make healing a priority. It is my hope that this book will reach those who need to hear this message. Would you be interested in helping someone you may not know? If so I have an ask to make for someone you do not know. The way to get this message to those who need to start their healing journey is by reaching them. Most do judge a book by its cover and reviews. If you have found this book helpful thus far would you take a brief moment right now to leave an honest review of this book and its contents? It will cost you zero dollars and less than 1 minute. Your review will help someone out there who suffers from anxiety. It will not only help one person but everyone around them. Your review will help one more person find peace in their life. Your review will help one more person find self-love and inner peace in their life. You could be the one review that can help someone completely start transforming their life. To make this happen all you have to do is take less than 1 minute and leave a review.

HOW TO FIND INSTANT PEACE

This too shall pass.

— PERSIAN ADAGE

Y ou know that feeling of complete and total defeat, when the deadline is ten minutes away and you still have about three hours of work to do? By this point, your options are either give up or fail. So what do you do when you face this problem? You first need to find calm amid the storm. Finding instant peace sounds great but before it becomes instant, it takes work to find it, and then instantly access it.

Peace in life comes with knowing that you are going to feel every emotion that comes with being human. It means feeling everything, even what we perceive as good and as bad. Anxiety tries to get us to push down our emotions or deal with it at a later stage, or it tries to get us to linger in the emotions for as long as possible, until there is nothing more that we can do than just call it what it is—unhealthy.

If you look at something like procrastination, this is a great example of how prolonging or living in the past can be detrimental to us. When we procrastinate, we put off a task that would have probably taken us 20 minutes to complete. But for some reason, we avoid doing the task and we keep postponing and putting it off for a later stage. We can procrastinate because we don't want to do it right now, we don't like the project itself, we don't like the person we need to work with, or it just seems way too overwhelming, and so what we do is we find other things to do in the meantime that prevents us from getting into the thick of it.

We do smaller tasks that we enjoy, we do things that are not as pressing or as urgent, or we just do completely random things that are neither necessary nor beneficial, like scrolling through social media or cleaning our oven. We use this as a way of procrastinating and the whole day we carry the burden of this one task on our shoulders. It stays with us, present in our mind, tainting everything that we do, because we chose not to attend to it when we could. And then more things happen, emergencies come up, and when you told yourself you'd get to it at 4:00 p.m., you suddenly realize that urgent work came up that is now due at 4:30 p.m. Now you can't get that one small task done, because you left it for later, your stress and anxiety has built up, and you don't know what more to do to ease the panic. When you do get around to eventually doing the task, you realize that it only takes you ten minutes to do and you find the frustration staying with you for a long time afterwards as well. By leaving a task for later, we just have so much more to deal with than addressing it right away in the moment.

The same thing happens with unpleasant feelings. In her TEDx talk in 2016, clinician Dr. Joan Rosenberg states that if you choose to be fully present in a moment, you are aware rather than avoiding. Does this sound familiar? It sounds a lot like mindfulness, right? Well, Dr. Rosenberg states that we need to make a choice to be fully present in a moment that is presented to us with pleasant or unpleasant emotions. When you choose to distract yourself or avoid what you are feeling, this feeling stays with us for a long time because it constantly takes effort to push it down, or because we wallow in the feeling (TEDx, 2016). Does this sound familiar? It sounds a lot like anxiety, right?

Dr. Rosenberg states that the best way to deal with emotions is to stay present and deal with whatever emotions we feel right there and then. This is the same for good emotions and bad emotions. But what exactly are bad emotions? Do these even exist? The reality is that there are no bad emotions, just unpleasant emotions. There are eight unpleasant emotions. These are sadness, shame, helplessness, anger, embarrassment, disappointment, frustration, and vulnerability. These feelings are not negative or bad, they are just unpleasant or uncomfortable. And just like anxiety, we may try to avoid these feelings. We are afraid of experiencing these uncomfortable feelings because we have the fear that they may never go away, that they are going to be too intense and overwhelming, or that we may lose control when faced with these feelings. But our emotional strength is directly correlated and linked with our ability to fully feel an unpleasant emotion, and move through that unpleasant emotion (TEDx, 2016).

Our emotions are manifested physically and physiologically. Exhibit A, anxiety (emotion) leads to shaking and a sped up heart rate (physical) because of the stress hormones that our brain releases (physiological). The real motivating factor between why we try to avoid unpleasant and uncomfortable feelings is because we don't like the physical feeling, we don't like the physical sensations in our body that these emotions evoke. The solution to this, according to Dr. Rosenberg, is to just experience the emotion in the moment, right there and then. Emotions come in waves, and she advises that you just ride the wave. You see, feelings, both good and bad, only last between 60 and 90 seconds, from the moment the emotion triggers a physiological response in your brain to the moment it dissipates out of our system. That's it. Just 90 seconds. So when you let your emotion sit with you and you allow it ruin your entire day, you are allowing a 90 second response to control your entire day. It may seem like negative emotions last longer than positive emotions, but that is because the human mind, for years and years, has been more inclined to focus on the negative, because knowing the bad helps us survive. "Bad" emotions teach us what to avoid and that's why it seems to hold a stronger resonance in our minds. But the reality is that for all emotions that we all experience almost everyday, 90 seconds is the time it lasts.

Dr. Rosenberg, through her theory that has been dubbed The Rosenberg Reset, states that you should be fully present and mindful in the moment that you experience your emotions. Ride the wave, feel it and experience it entirely, so that when the moment passes, you can easily let go of that feeling. The beauty is that you can rest in the fact that the emotions will pass and it won't control you for longer than it needs to. Some emotions come in many waves, following after each other constantly. This is so clearly seen in the form of grief where we experience emotions over and over again. But if you stay present in the moment of extreme emotion, and you deal with the 90 seconds of emotions, you will get through it and feel better even sooner.

If you face these emotions in the moment, you can deal with them, and overcome them in a better and well-adjusted way. This then allows you the opportunity to unhook from past trauma that are associated with the negative emotions you experienced in the past that served as a reminder and a persistent nuisance feeling. By mastering the power of being fully present when experiencing your emotions, you can experience instant relief and instant peace from those emotions. After facing your 90 second reaction, you are on your way to freedom and peace.

Once again, this is a way that mindfulness allows you to completely immerse yourself into the current emotion, so that you feel it fully, you get over it immediately, and you feel instant peace. Without the bitter taste left in your mouth, there is no space for anxiety to linger around because you have faced those emotions head on.

MAKING IT A HABIT

So now that you know how to overcome the powerful emotions that we as humans experience almost on a daily basis, you're probably going to tell me that I'm insane because it is so easy to fall back into the habit of lingering and dwelling in these emotions. How do you stop this? It's quite easy. You make it a habit.

You have probably heard that it takes around 21 days to form a habit. But the reality is that developing and sticking with a habit is different for everyone. Gyming is one of the most common habits that we see people trying to form. But the purpose of the habit gets lost on many. Going to the gym is a tool that people use to achieve healthier lifestyles. I have seen people take out gym memberships and they seem to develop lifelong habits of going to the gym religiously in just one week. I have seen people go to the gym for three months, and eventually fall back into their old habits and stop going to the gym completely.

The thing is, if we don't make changes in our routines, then we won't see changes in our mindset. The goal is to create and form habits that set us on a path of happiness, joy, and peace. When you live with depression and anxiety, you slowly but surely develop habits to support those feelings of depression and anxiety. Basically what you feed is what will gain strength. If you feed your depression and anxiety with negative habits, then that is what will grow. Mindful habits, on the other hand, bring our minds to a state of conscious joy.

Forming a habit is not just about developing an act, but rather about knowing what the purpose of that act is. It's not that you want to stop eating chocolate, it's rather that you want to lower your cholesterol and blood sugar, so limiting chocolate is the tool you use.

There are three rules that you can follow to establish habits (Clear, 2014):

1. The first rule is that you need to start with something that is small enough that you have no excuse not to do it, and that it's not difficult enough that you try getting out of doing it.
2. The next rule is that you need to be able to gradually increase this task each day without noticing too much of a change. So you are not going to make great proclamations that set unrealistic goals for yourself and ultimately set you up for failure.

3. The third rule is that even though you increase your task or the habit you are hoping to build, repeating this task each day should continue to remain easy and achievable. The second it becomes too hard, you are going to be tempted to give up. By making a change that is almost unnoticeable, you can continue as you have been, while still achieving growth and an increase.

With meditation, your habit would start with a minute a day. I know, you're busy, you have too many things to do. But if you take away one minute from scrolling on your phone and you use that minute to engage in mindful meditation, you will be doing yourself a favor without taking away from the importance of the tasks you need to complete.

Each day, you can increase this minute by five seconds, which in reality may seem like nothing but eventually you find yourself basking in the joy of a 10-minute meditation session. However, 10 minutes in one go may seem like it's eating into your clock, so you can begin creating ways of splitting this time up (Clear, 2014).

Overcoming your anxiety and depression is unlocked by simply practicing each and every day—you practice mindfulness, you strengthen your mind each day by actively trying to rewire your thought process, you create a space for yourself where you can safely work through your emotions in the moment they occur rather than leaving them for later or trying to avoid them completely.

Practice Gratitude

On your journey to mindfulness, we cannot overlook the role of gratitude. You know what it feels like to have someone say "thank you" to you, but have you ever wondered what gratitude means to someone else? And I don't mean what it does for them, giving them an ego boost and making them feel good, but what it does for you to show gratitude. Often, our thank yous are empty and said from a place of need instead of from a deep and meaningful place. But gratitude, when sincere, can do amazing things for your mental health.

Studies have found gratitude to be extremely beneficial to those who are both neurologically typical, as well as those who face depression and anxiety, or are in need of some sort of mental health counseling.

In 2017, a study conducted by Brown and Wong sought to see what the benefit of gratitude would be in those who were in need of mental health counseling. At this point, research had mostly focused on well-functioning individuals. This study looked at three different groups:

one which was instructed to write letters of gratitude to any recipient (even though the letters were not mailed), the other group was instructed to write about their deepest thoughts and negative feelings, and the last group, serving as the control group, was not required to complete a writing task. All three groups did receive counseling (Brown & Wong, 2017).

The results that were found were astonishing and the role of gratitude was shown to be beneficial to the person showing gratitude even though they had not sent the letters to the recipient. This in itself shows that gratitude, even if it is never received, is beneficial to the person giving gratitude. This can therefore be seen as an emotion, a feeling, or a trait that fills the giver—showing gratitude doesn't take anything away from you but also fills your emotional and mental cup.

This study uncovered some wonderful findings (Brown & Wong, 2017):

1. The first thing that was found was that words have power. Because of how amazing our brain works, the language that we use has the power to overcome mental health problems. Letters that were written from a point of gratitude contained more positive words, as expected, and those written from a place of deep hurt and

negative emotions contained more negative words. While being positive doesn't directly lead to prolonged and better mental health in the long term, a reduction of negative words and negativity does. This means that an increase in positivity must be accompanied by a decrease in negativity for it to have long lasting positive mental health effects. And when gratitude is your focus, your brain is preoccupied with positivity, leading to an almost automatic decrease in negative thoughts. When your mind is so full of goodness, happiness, and thankfulness, you don't have much capacity left to be focused on sadness and negativity.

2. The second thing this study found was that gratitude is beneficial to you even if you don't share it. It is the gift that keeps on giving and if you share it, you never get depleted.

3. The third thing that was found was that, much like with mindfulness, the effects of mental health are not instant. Instead, if you start showing gratitude a little bit each day, you may not overcome your stress and anxiety immediately, but in the long run, you will notice an extreme change in your general

outlook toward life. This is part of forming a new habit, a habit of gratitude and positivity.

4. Lastly, this study also found that gratefulness has a long lasting effect in the brain of those who display gratitude habitually. This study found that those who paid something forward to someone that they were thankful for experienced greater neural sensitivity in the medial prefrontal cortex, a brain area associated with learning and decision making (Brown & Wong, 2017). This shows how this one simple act can rewire your entire brain.

What can we learn from this study and from practicing gratitude? We learn that simply by building a habit of gratitude we can make some astronomical changes in our lives and in our brains.

ESCAPING THE CYCLE

Insanity is defined as doing the same thing over again and expecting a different outcome.

— ALBERT EINSTEIN

S o we know that anxiety occurs in a cycle, and sometimes when you have worked through getting over anxiety, you may still feel like you're completely stuck. And though you're dealing with your anxiety, you don't feel like you're overcoming it. This can add to the stress and anxiety rather than help it. You may feel like you're trying the same thing over and over again, only to end up in the position, stuck, facing the anxiety that you seem to have become so familiar with.

This can begin making you feel demotivated and like you're stuck. My first piece of advice in this case would be to reassess the methods that you are using to try and escape your anxiety cycle. Whether you are doing mindful practices, breathing practices, or using herbal supplements, we have already seen that each person is different. A solution that I swear by is something that may not even mildly work for you. Whether you are making a complete change in the way you try to over-come your anxiety, or if you are slightly tweaking what you have already been doing, a change is needed. From my experience, people that are usually coming off from anxiety medication that have been prescribed to them by professionals, find themselves seeping back into old routines and getting sucked back into their anxiety.

The next thing you will need to do is become entirely familiar with and recognize the anxiety cycle so that you can figure out where you are stuck in the cycle and so you can figure out ways of getting out of the anxiety cycle. This is something I like to call the Trojan Horse. Basically, you learn to recognise your anxiety cycle so well that you are able to either immediately stop what you have been facing or develop strategies that work well enough for you to get out of that point.

But this is not just about knowing the four stages and having an overview or understanding on how to escape from each. This is about knowing how this applies to you and your own personal distress that you face with anxiety.

In order to successfully recognise which stage you are in in the anxiety cycle, you first need to know the stages, and you need to know what is your own personal response to each stage. Let's briefly recap what the stages are. Stage one is feeling anxious, recognizing the feeling, and almost immediately seeking ways to overcome the anxiety. Stage two: suddenly, a solution presents itself, in the form of avoidance. Stage three is that almost instant sense of relief knowing that you have dodged a bullet and now you're over the anxiety, but uh-oh, stage four is realizing that the trigger you avoided is still there waiting for you to face it. It is then that you realize that avoidance was just a temporary solution (Mandriota, 2022).

So now that you know what each stage in the anxiety cycle is, you now need to figure out where you are in the anxiety cycle. Although it is an emotional response, there are physical manifestations of what you are feeling on the inside that will show on the outside. Most often, the first stage of the anxiety cycle will be that instant fight-or-flight response. Before I give you an everyday anxiety example, I want to give you an unrealistic and entirely dramatized version, just so you can accurately see the range in which you can experience the fight-or-flight response. Let's say you're camping in the woods and you see a bear. You stop dead in your tracks. You are unsure if they have seen you, but you know they smelled you. You see them slowly come towards you. Your heart is pounding in your chest, your ears are ringing, your legs feel like jelly, and you have broken out into a sweat that covers every inch of your body.

Immediately, your brain starts analyzing the situation at hand. You look around for a weapon, but you know that man vs bear has a clear winner and a clear loser. You know the bear is going to begin charging at you at any point, so you start scoping the area—is there a tree that you can climb, shelter you can hide in, and if so what is its proximity to you in relation to the bear you are going to be facing. In the moment, you decide to "flight" because your "fight" is not an option. Now, as I said, this is not a realistic situation, but it most certainly is the worst anxiety-inducing response you could face. This is on one extreme of the scale.

Now let's look at a more realistic example. Let us say that, for example, you suffer from some form of social anxiety, whether you are aware of it or not. You are invited to a party where there is probably going to be more than ten people in the room. Your comfort level stops at three people. What makes this scenario worse is that most of the ten people that are going to be there are people you don't know. Now, this can go one of two ways: the first is that you decide to go (fight), but before you do, you numb the anxiety by throwing back a few drinks to face the feelings that you know are going to shortly flood your body—the sweat, the pounding heart, and the weak knees. Indirectly, you are also using alcohol to *avoid* these feelings. The second option is that you decide you are not going to attend. You avoid the situation entirely and, afterwards, you breathe in a welcomed sigh of relief. But this avoidance makes your world smaller, and guess what? Your friend decided to reschedule the party and now you're expected to attend again in two weeks time.

When you are in the first stage of the anxiety cycle, you are directly met with an immediate need to decide on whether to fight or flight. It is an automatic response, and it happens whether you actively make the decision or not, and whether you're completely aware of it or not. In the second stage of the anxiety cycle, you will have all the physical manifestations of anxiety which is what leads you to avoid the situation at hand. The last stage is what leaves you feeling mentally and emotionally exhausted.

The way that you can determine which anxiety stage you are currently in is by answering three questions. The first is what sets off the feeling of anxiety? Was it an event, a memory, a person? This is, in fact, you identifying what your trigger is.

The next question you are going to ask yourself is what was your first reaction to the trigger you experienced? Were you excited, were you met with dread and fear, or were you completely indifferent?

The last question you are going to ask yourself is what did you do at the moment? What was your action that was in response to your reaction?

If you find yourself knowing that you have been triggered, chances are you are still in the first stage of the anxiety cycle. If you find that you are feeling fear or dread, chances are you are in the second stage of the anxiety cycle, and if you haven't responded to the situation at hand, you may not have made it to the final stage as yet. But if you find yourself avoiding the situation, and feeling instant relief from what you would have faced, then you have made it to the last stage of the cycle (Mandriota, 2022).

When you are faced with a response to any stage of the anxiety cycle, you are going to take an intel of your body and what you are experiencing in that moment.

You are going to be MINDFUL. Take a tally of your thoughts, are you making things seem worse than they actually are? Are you catastrophizing the situation? What are your physical responses that you are experiencing? And lastly, how did you mentally respond to the situation (Mandriota, 2022)?

There are steps that you can take to stop the cycle in its tracks, which involves being aware and mindful of how you react and respond to each stage. You first gain power in combating the anxiety cycle by knowing that you are in an anxiety cycle, and then you try to reverse each stage that you may be in. So it is quite clear by this point that to reverse a certain stage within the stress cycle, you would obviously need to be aware or knowledgable about where you are to combat it. That is why so much emphasis is paid on knowing your response to the anxiety cycle.

So how do you reverse each step of the anxiety cycle? Allow me to explain: in the first stage of the anxiety cycle, are you using any form of unhealthy coping mechanism to deal with the anxiety that you are faced with? Are you considering drinking something before heading to the party or are you considering canceling and avoiding the event altogether? In the second stage of the cycle, you are going to need to allow yourself to face the anxiety you were feeling. Hear me out, I'm not saying you need to live with anxiety forever, but what I'm saying is that instead of experiencing shallow and short-term relief for the anxiety, instead face the anxiety head on for a short period of time. Next, you are going to find healthy coping mechanisms to deal with the anxiety that you know you experience. And lastly, while this may take some time to grasp, you are slowly going to realize that you have the ability to take control of the situation at hand rather than allowing the situation and the anxiety to control you (Mandriota, 2022).

When you realize that the same approach you have been using towards anxiety has been keeping you trapped in the anxiety cycle, that is when you can have the courage to change what it is that you are facing, take back control of your mind, and find the strength that lies within.

ANXIETY REDUCING HABITS

If you are reading this book, I think it is safe to say that now, or at some point, you have suffered from an anxiety disorder. And chances are, the reason why you are trying to combat this anxiety disorder is because of the feelings that anxiety causes within you. The discomfort, the pain, the misery, all of it is what we fear and what we hope to never feel. On your journey towards reducing and combating anxiety, there are some habits that you can develop to help you fight anxiety.

According to Deanne Repich, Director of the National Institute of Anxiety and Stress, there are six habits that you can form to combat your anxiety (Repich, n.d.):

1. Acknowledge your anxiety. The more you try to hide the fact that you suffer from anxiety, the more you create the perception that anxiety is something wrong and that needs to be hidden. Why do we hide things? We hide them because we are ashamed, embarrassed, or afraid of them. If you are choosing not to acknowledge your anxiety, you create shame, fear, and embarrassment of this anxiety. You give your anxiety power! Instead, acknowledge and admit your feelings, first to yourself, and then to someone else—whether it is a friend, a family member, or even a stranger.

2. Find ways to combat stress immediately and in the long run. Remember that mindfulness is the long game. If you feel that you can't live with the crippling anxiety, while working towards long term mechanisms, you can also use natural supplements to ease the pain of anxiety.

3. Use power language. Words hold power, and how you talk to yourself holds even more power. You can either decide to be the victim or to hold the power, and each will be determined by the words you use toward yourself. Victim language asks "why does this always happen to me?" "I just can't seem to get past this challenge in my life." "I'm never going to get past this." "Things should have worked out differently." Victim language never does any good. It traps you in a black hole of negativity. Instead, use powerful language to remind yourself of everything you can do!

4. Work on your inner strength. Once you find your inner strength, each day you get to work a little harder and harder on flexing this strength, over your worries, your stress, and over your anxiety. In the end, you find yourself being stronger and being more powerful over your thoughts and your actions. But it is a daily excuse. Why do bodybuilders go to the gym everyday? It's because they don't want to lose any of the muscle mass they have worked so hard towards achieving. The same goes for your mind.

5. Start small. Don't set yourself up for failure, increased stress, and prolonged anxiety by

creating unrealistic expectations for yourself. Break everything up into smaller goals that you are hoping to achieve, and this will give you a better sense of accomplishment. Don't decide to meditate for an hour everyday. It's unrealistic. Start with a minute or two minutes each day.

6. Decide to start now. There is always a better time or a warmer day to do something. Tomorrow always seems like the better option when you're searching to make beneficial changes for yourself. Stop postponing, stop dwelling in your anxiety, and start working towards a better version of yourself immediately. You know how people always want to start diets on a Monday? Don't postpone your mental well being (Repich, n.d.).

Practicing these habits everyday is a sure way of getting yourself established in a mentally healthier routine and you will find yourself combating the very thing that seemed to control your life. You never have to hand the reins over to anxiety anymore. Instead, you get to be in the driver's seat and you get to be in control. Isn't that amazing?

BUILDING YOUR ARMOR
AGAINST ANXIETY

Never forget what you are, the rest of the world will not. Wear it like armor and it can never be used to hurt you.

— GEORGE R. R. MARTIN

So now that you know how to overcome anxiety, you may think that you're somewhat of a pro, ready to kick anxiety in the butt and head on to greener pastures. But your journey is far from over.

Throughout this book, the theme of habits, forming habits, and sticking to habits have become extremely prominent. But having good and healthy habits in place are one of the best ways of defending yourself against the scourge of anxiety. Habits form such a large part of our lives. As human beings, habits are what keep us thriving. But it can also lead to our failure. We form habits in almost every way—from doing morning meditation, to eating a greasy burger with bacon to cure a hangover. Habits from a foundational element of human life. We develop habits to exercise, but we also form unhealthy habits, like scrolling through social media when we're supposed to be working, or drinking and smoking. But the habits that we form are only as strong as the motivation we have to stick to these habits.

I am someone who is extremely motivated by chips and for chips. If you want me to do anything at all, I don't care about a monetary incentive or even a fancy vacation. But you promise me a bag of chips, you can guarantee that the task will be done to your utmost satisfaction. I love chips so much that I have formed a habit around when I purchase and eat chips—it's usually late at night when my kids are fast asleep and I don't need to share with anyone. But this is an unhealthy habit. A habit nonetheless, but I know that eating chips is not a healthy snack to consume. I have also often found myself wondering what my reaction would be if my kids ate as much chips as I do, and the answer is that I would be utterly and completely upset.

But if I won't allow them to have this habit because it's unhealthy, then why do I allow myself to do it?

While this is one of my more unhealthy habits, I have created a healthier habit of eating at least one fruit a day and doing my daily meditation first thing in the morning. Forming this habit wasn't as easy as the chips one, but I witnessed the results and the benefits I experienced after forming this habit and that motivated me to stick with it. Thereafter it was like leveling up in a game, where the more I did, the better I felt, which was motivation to do more.

Habits are hard to form. And the reason why they are hard to form is because we often have no idea how to form a habit. Habits usually start on a new years' eve with a sweeping declaration about what you're planning to do *everyday* for the *rest of the year*. By doing this, you are unfortunately setting yourself up for failure, despite the good intentions you have. It is unrealistic that you are going to stick to the habit you have created for yourself especially when any possible goal you set for yourself is almost unattainable.

Let's imagine that your habits are a buffet meal that is just overflowing with all types of magnificent deliciousness. You see the feast before your eyes and you know you need to try everything. So you fill your plate up with a little bit of everything. When you start eating, you start with one little bite at a time. You don't toss everything straight into your mouth and eat it all in one go. You may even find yourself going back day after day, trying something different each time because you know you can't try everything in one sitting. The same goes for the habits that you form. You need to start small and work your way up. Don't jump in the deep end because you are setting yourself up for failure.

So why do you need to start with tiny habits? Because as humans, anything difficult requires a certain amount of motivation. And if we don't have the motivation, the chances are that we are not going to do something. If motivation becomes the factor that pushes you to form a habit, then you are setting yourself up for failure. Let's be honest, even chefs lose their motivation to cook everyday, and cooking is what they are supposed to be passionate about. If they lack motivation on some days, you can only imagine how little motivation I have more often (Start Tiny, n.d.).

But when a behavior is easy and small enough to complete without it even taking any time in our day, it is a lot easier to stick to. Creating or establishing a solid habit is not about going big, or even about doing it properly. It's just about starting. It's about creating a space and a time in your life for the habit. There's no excuse to miss out on morning meditation when you find yourself automatically awake after 5:00 a.m. Once you find time in your life for a small habit, that time in your life becomes earmarked or dedicated to that habit. Which makes it easier to grow that habit because you don't have the excuse of saying there's no time.

Despite how small and how easy these habits may be, you need to start somewhere. And in reality, that is the hardest part. So how do you establish a habit? How do you become a person who appears to have it all together? Well, you're first going to set very specific goals with very specific objectives in mind. Don't say you want to exercise everyday. Say that you want to exercise for 10 minutes every morning. Removing ambiguity makes the goal easier to hold onto. Knowing what you're hoping to get from your goal is also a great way of making sure you maintain your daily habit. But again, you're going to start small. You're not going to say that you want to lose 20 lbs, instead you're going to start with 2 lbs, or you're going to say you want to be healthier. Saying that you want to start a healthy habit to also be someone that others look up to and wonder how you keep it all together, I'm afraid, is not a good motivation (Milkman, 2021).

Next, you need to develop a cue-based plan. This means that you will need something to serve as a trigger or as an encouragement that pushes you to work on your habit. Something that works for me is as simple as a daily alarm that reminds me that now is the time to work on my habit. I know that an alarm might seem distracting, especially when you're in the middle of something. So what I do is set two alarms—one as a fifteen minute reminder, and one as the actual start alarm. This allows me to finish up what I am doing or get to a natural stopping point before starting on my habit (Milkman, 2021).

The third thing you'd want to do is make your habit fun. It needs to be something you look forward to doing rather than something that you actually dread doing. This will make it easier to stick to in the long term. When you start forming habits, you really need to acknowledge and focus on the good things that are happening in your day. Even if it is one small good feeling you have had. This helps reinforce the positivity of the changes you are making, which in turn will rein-force building life changing habits. The secret to enjoying your habit is making sure that it aligns up with your end goal. If you want fast results, then do something that is quick and enjoyable, not something that puts way too much strain on you.

It's easy to form a habit, and when your body clicks into autopilot, your routine is set. But if you add some flexibility into your routine, especially when you start off, you allow yourself to be subliminally prepared for when your routine is thrown off track. We all have those disastrous mornings where nothing seems to go as planned. Having the option of flexibility allows you to still make sure you stick to forming your habit, even on these mornings. When you use these elements to form your habit, you'll find it easy and you'll find yourself wondering why you didn't do it sooner. The reality is that you could have done it sooner, but the idea of habit formation seemed too complicated in your mind to begin with.

Forming a habit is the first step in equipping yourself against fighting anxiety and depression. But how does this happen? Small habits usually result in big lifestyle change, and it usually happens so gradually that you don't even notice it has occurred. It makes you feel really good about yourself, and it honestly is like a gift to yourself. Aside from implementing the above mentioned steps to create and grow your habit successfully, you also need to celebrate your successes. Making the decision to do something beneficial to you is an amazing accomplishment, and sticking with it is even greater. So commend yourself on making it thus far. Instead of taking a step in the right direction, you have taken five steps into the right direction.

OUT WITH THE OLD

Now that you know how to form a habit, you need to know exactly what type of habits will help you directly overcome your anxiety. Because let's be honest, drinking less coffee might ease your anxiety, but it's not a habit that is going to immediately reduce your anxiety.

The first habit you can form is the habit of talking about what it is you're going through. As soon as you realize that those that are close to you will help you through the difficulties you face, the quicker you can get out of the mindset that anxiety is a taboo or a bad thing. The reality is that everyone fights an unseen battle, and whether anxiety is your biggest or your only battle, sometimes just talking about it helps you feel like you are not alone.

The next next clink in your armor that you are going to patch up is that of physical exercise. I know the feeling all too well, of sitting behind your desk from morning until evening, constantly working, and having no time to do any form of movement because you are scared of missing even a single second of work. But as humans, we were not meant to sit behind a desk for eight hours. We are meant to move. I'm not saying go full force into lifting heavy weights, but start with movement and flexibility training. And if you can do any form of exercise outside, well then you have hit the jackpot. Try to get some time in nature on a daily basis, and if you can kill two birds with one stone by exercising outside, you are good to go.

We have already covered the other important habits that help you overcome anxiety like mindfulness, gratefulness, and journaling. But something that gets overlooked are your sleeping habits. Many people are all over the show with their sleeping habits, working until late, and falling asleep with their computer near them. Am I talking from experience? I might be. Sleeping is so important that we dedicate a third of our lives to it. We can therefore safely assume that it is worth it to do it properly.

Another healthy habit you can form is finding time for self-care. We all too often allow our self-care to fall by the wayside. I am not encouraging procrastination in the name of self-care or missing deadlines because you were too busy doing something for yourself. Instead what I am saying is that you set a realistic amount of time aside each week or each month to do something entirely selfish. If you are a mom, this may look like getting a babysitter and heading out for a massage. It may look like booking yourself a room for one night to get away from the routine of everyday life, or it may look like a long luxurious bath while reading your favorite book. Whatever it is, it is important and you need to do it. Replenish yourself!

And finally, two habits that will do you good even if you don't suffer from anxiety are keeping things clean and decluttered, and limiting your screen time. Let's look at decluttering. When your space is running havoc on you, you can be sure that your mind will be as frazzled as your surroundings. Forming a healthy habit can look like decluttering your workspace before you actually begin working. This allows you to be the best functioning version of yourself. If I am sitting at a cluttered and disorganized work space, I find myself paying an unusual amount of attention to the clutter and trying to move things around instead of working. By starting with decluttering, I remove the distraction, and I remove any anxiety that is caused by delays to my workflow.

The next thing is screen time. No one needs to tell us how toxic screen time and social media is, and yet we seem drawn to it. Social media posts are not meant to control our emotions the way they do. It is not healthy nor normal to be crying at a post one minute, then laughing the next minute because of something you see on social media. That is tampering with our emotions in an unhealthy way. Limiting screen time does a lot of good for your mental health. I know it seems strange that social media can trigger our anxiety, but when you see someone who is your age and that seems to have accomplished so much more in life, it may make you feel like you are "behind" in life. This can make you feel anxious about wanting to do more than you can actually handle. Also, the second you feel like you desire a staged version of life, you can realize that you are doing something unhealthy. Nothing on social media is reality. Instead, it is a small version of reality, it is the part that people choose to share. By wanting this, you are hoping for an unrealistic version of life, a version that can never be achieved, and that you will ultimately fail at achieving. I'm not telling you to delete all social media apps from your device, because that is not realistic either. Just limit yourself to the time you spend on social media. The reality is that social media is our go-to when we are bored. Instead, dedicate ten minutes during your lunch break to scroll through social media. Then you can count the rest of your would-be social media time as free time and you'd be surprised at what you can accomplish in those moments.

Something I find extremely interesting, that I have done this myself, and that I highly recommend is to set your phone's screen time report and show notifications to see the reports. This will help you raise awareness of how much time is actually spent on your phone. A few years ago, before I went off social media for good, I set my screen time notifications. I was in the process of building habits, I was waking up an hour earlier to fit in body movement, meditation, and journaling. I had built up these habits and wanted more time for them, because it truly felt like being at a spa for me. But I really didn't want to wake up another hour earlier. Being aware of wanting more time for "me," it dawned on me… How do I manage to get four hours of screen time a day? It was so crazy that 15 minutes here and 15 minutes there ended up consuming more than four hours a day! It seems obvious writing it now, but I simply wasn't aware of where I was putting my time and energy. Once I became aware, I was able to acknowledge, work on it, and replace idleness with something beneficial. In being aware and being mindful, you will find doors that will open to make healthy adjustments.

All of these small little habits are a sure way of reducing your overall anxiety. But the key is to be realistic with yourself—with the time it will take to see a change in your anxiety and with how much time you can dedicate to each habit. Also remember that it is not realistic to expect yourself to do all of these habits. You may not even like some of them. But if you start with one a day for five minutes of the day, you are on the right track. Starting is the hardest part after all.

Find Your Groove

I love a good routine. A morning routine, a bath time routine, an evening routine, and a good skin-care routine. I love it all. And once I have added something into my routine, I know I'm sticking to it for good. You can also bet that if I get taken away from my routine, I am going to be grumpy about it. You see, I like being in control of my routine. I like knowing what I can expect to happen.

But, as I have mentioned, each person is different. There are others who hate the idea of predictability. They are the people whose creative juices flow more when they change the environment or they take a different approach to their everyday tasks. However, despite what works best for you, it has been proven that during times of stress and anxiety, it is best to have a routine in place. When you are facing a stressful situation, you may find yourself uncertain on how to cope with what is happening around you. Your mind becomes fixated on what is not in your control and since it's out of your control, there is absolutely nothing you can do about it.

When control is immediately taken away from you, it causes us to feel like everything we know has been taken and turned on its head. That is why, whether you are a routine person or not, it is always great to follow some form of consistency during times of anxiety and stress. This is the time for you to control what's within your means to control. Plan what you're going to eat for lunch—heck, plan what you're going to eat tomorrow and the day after too.

Developing a routine, not only during times of stress, but even on a daily basis reduces stress, helps you develop and stick to your habits, it allows you to take time to care for yourself (which often falls by the wayside), you can feel more productive, and you can feel more focused on the tasks at hand. Now, this is beneficial whether you are following a strict routine with an hour by hour breakdown, or even if you are following a loose to-do list that maps out the tasks that you need to do during the day (Cherry, 2020).

If we think about our routines and how closely we stick to them, they are essentially the sum total of all the habits we have formed throughout our lives. Our routines will reflect whether or not we have healthy or unhealthy habits.

But remember that when you attempt to create new routines and forge new habits, you need to be patient with yourself. The best way to establish healthy habits is by being mindful of the tasks and actions you are hoping to consistently pursue. In practicing mindfulness, learn to accept the feelings you experience in the moment. Don't try to fight it and don't try to alter it. You will accept them because the good emotions are reinforcing good habits, the uncomfortable emotions are telling you to make changes. In being patient with yourself and being mindful of your feelings, being uncomfortable is an opportunity to ask yourself, "Am I uncomfortable because this is new? Will this discomfort help me in the long run, or do I need to make small adjustments to help ease the discomfort?" Awareness brings up these conversations within ourselves, conversations that we need to have to keep us on the right track.

7

BABY STEPS

The thing is, each one of us is the sum total of every moment that we've ever experienced, with all the people we've ever known.

— LEO, *THE VOW*

L et us start with an exercise. For a moment, just close your eyes and think back on your life. Allow your mind to run back, tracing its hand along all the memories you hold dear to you. While we may not recall the everyday memories of taking showers and heading to work or school, instead, we will see, almost as highlights, all the major moments of our lives. Allow yourself to think back on all these highlighted moments —the moments that stand out. Why do they stand out for you? Are they good memories or bad memories?

Whether they are good memories or bad memories, our minds bookmark them to think back on, either to remember the feeling of the memory, or to think back on how events unfolded. Whatever the memories are, there is a reason why they are highlighted by our brains. The pleasant and the unpleasant memories are all important aspects of who we are. But these big moments are a culmination of all the small events that led up to these big moments.

Allow me to divulge. The big positive moments for me are the birth of my kids. But giving birth was just the culmination of many small moments that led to my kids entering the world. This moment was made up of a positive pregnancy test, a first scan, a first heartbeat, a gender reveal, feeling tiny little kicks and tiny little movements, sharing the news with loved ones, and lastly, giving birth to the little bundle I waited so long for.

So when you think back on what makes you who you are, I think we can all safely agree that we did not wake up one day and achieve something big. Instead, the big things took time to work towards. The news of your promotion did not come one random day unexpectedly. You worked day in and day out towards achieving the promotion. And if the promotion wasn't directly your goal, you still earned it by consistently working hard towards it.

But what contributes to these big moments that we experience throughout our lives? Quite simply put, it is our habits and what we do that make up the big moments. I can guarantee you that no one in the world has experienced the exact same moment you have. This is because, what makes us who we are, what comprises the majority of our daily activity and routine is our habits. And the chances of our habits matching someone else's exactly is zero to one.

We have spoken about our daily routines and how beneficial they can be. But at its most basic level, our routines are made up entirely of our habits. Our habits are things that we do from muscle-memory. They are automatic responses that we have been doing religiously and consistently all the time until they became second nature to us. This second nature actually becomes our default setting and it becomes our autopilot mode. Studies in cognitive psychology and neurobiology have found that about 40% to 95% of our human behavior is habitual (Walesh, n.d.). This means that for the most part of our day, far more than half of our day, is made up of us moving in autopilot mode. If our days are met almost entirely with our habits, we best make sure they are good habits.

Imagine if the way you faced each day was with confidence, positivity, and thankfulness? Well, now we know that this is a possibility provided you form the right habits (which makes up our routine and our responses to each day). But you're probably wondering how habits can help us when our stimuli around us don't really evoke positive responses. Once again, our habits will help us respond appropriately and accordingly.

Building small habits gives you confidence but it's all about starting small. Even if you're just being grateful for the meal you're about to eat. We have already seen the benefits of being grateful, and that's really how small it needs to be to start. It's kind of like building a house. You don't wake up one morning to a fully built house. You don't even wake up and make the decision to build the entire house in one day. Instead, brick by brick, you put in the effort and create the masterpiece you have hoped for. You see a dream become a reality. The same goes for the way you build yourself up and the traits you reflect. You start with the foundation— saying thank you to someone who gives you a glass of water. Brick by brick, you approach everything with a new found gratitude, you realize that in the world, you are not entitled to anything, and that everything that is done for you or given to you is not because someone has to, but because they choose to. And that in itself is reason enough to be grateful.

So how do you form healthy habits with baby steps? Well, if you're hoping to develop better sleeping habits, and you currently run on two to four hours of sleep each night, diving in head first into eight hours of sleep is going to leave you feeling so strange and it may even make you feel anxious because you feel like you're losing on four hours of your day. Instead, before trying to sleep for many hours in one night, try to find some consistency by taking the baby step of sleeping at the same time each night and waking up the same time each morning, on weekends as well (NEA Member Benefits, n.d.).

If you want to develop a habit of eating healthier, the baby step you can take is by replacing one unhealthy snack each day with a healthier one. If you're hoping to form healthy physical habits, you won't head straight into the gym and start lifting 100 lbs weights. Instead, take baby steps by parking on the far end of the shopping center, using the stairs instead of the elevator, or doing a few jumping jacks before you brush your teeth (NEA Member Benefits, n.d.).

Knowing that you need to build good habits is one thing. You have learnt over the past few chapters, the value and importance of developing habits that reduce and decrease your stress and anxiety. You have learnt the importance of mindfulness, thankfulness, and gratefulness. But one thing that we can unanimously agree on is that it is far easier to stick to an old habit than it is to form a new habit. And it's easy to stick to these bad habits even if they are bad habits. For example, why would you try to form healthier eating habits when you have a snack drawer right by your bedside drawer? Starting a new habit just seems like way too much effort: you have to make a trip to the store, buy healthy snacks, and then what would you do with all the candy bars and chips that are sitting in your snack drawer already? Even without me giving you these excuses, you know how easy it is to stick to a bad habit even though we know it's bad.

Personally, I very rarely buy chips at the store anymore because I know I don't just have a few chips—I eat the whole bag. If there are chips in the house, they will find me, or I will find them. We are drawn to each other, chips and I. I have acknowledged that when I crave chips, I ask myself why I didn't just buy some. But when that moment passes, I feel good about myself because I would not have felt good about myself if I mindlessly ate a few chips that ended up in the whole bag being gone. Every once in a while I grab a bag of chips to eat. But I am mindful about it!

In other words, I have found a way to set myself up for success by acknowledging my issue with chips. I have certain levels of strength at certain times of the day. At night, I formed a bad habit and I learned that time of weakness is a passing moment. At the moment I am frustrated, but overcoming the moment with preparation makes success far better and a longer lasting feeling that helps me continue with healthier eating habits.

In an attempt to create positive and healthy habits, we also need to unlearn and undo the bad habits that we have and that ultimately cause damage and blocks in our lives. Removing unhealthy and bad habits from our lives is extremely vital for us to work towards mindful versions of ourselves. Some habits lead us to be more anxious, and because we're so focused on our anxiety, we don't have the time nor the energy to focus on what is actually happening, we can't be present, we can't be mindful, and we can't be grateful. Essentially, bad habits prevent us from living in the moment. Let's look at some of the habits that make us feel stressed, anxious, and unproductive.

Despite when you were born, how old you are currently, and what it is you do with your life, the globe has faced extraordinarily high levels of stress and anxiety in recent years. We have seen so many global shifts happening, from a global pandemic, the great resignation, people changing career paths, adjusting to new jobs, dealing with the loss of loved ones, and even starting families in this extremely strange time that we live in. It goes without saying that everyone today is more stressed than they have been in the past. One of these bad habits that we need to undo is bad sleeping habits. It's strange though, now that many people work from home or that they have had to adjust to commuting back to work, people have to face working until late at night which means they are on their laptops until they sleep. This is one of the greatest bad habits that people face on a daily basis. Undoing bad sleeping habits can not only help you form and develop new habits, but it can also help you get to a healthier version of yourself by just taking away the bad stuff. In the case of bad sleeping habits, undoing the bad doesn't need to be replaced with a good habit. The bad habit just needs to be undone and you will immediately experience healthier outcomes (Beaton, 2016).

If you find that your mind, your stresses, and your anxiety is what is keeping you from sleeping well, you can keep a journal on your bed side to jot down the thoughts that plague you at night. The reality is that at 10:00 p.m. or 11:00 p.m., there is absolutely nothing you can do about the stresses that are twirling around in your mind or the great American novel idea that suddenly popped into your head. Instead, putting these thoughts on paper is the same as doing your brain dump first thing in the morning. It takes the pressure off you trying to remember, and you can properly address these thoughts at the appropriate time—when you're not meant to be asleep (Beaton, 2016).

Another unhealthy habit that we almost all fall victim to and that we need to actively work towards undoing is that of irregularly sustaining ourselves. We have all found ourselves claiming to be either too busy to eat, or too tired to eat, we skip breakfast because we're running late, or worse, thanks to the distorted idealization that society has created for us, we skip meals as a "quick-fix" to lose a few pounds. But while we think that we are just skipping a meal and nothing more, we are actually accelerating and propelling our anxiety into overdrive. The reason for this is because missing meals results in a chemical imbalance in our body that leads to low and unsteady blood sugar levels, the symptoms of which closely resemble the symptoms of anxiety. Your legs feel shaky, your heart pounds, and you feel dizzy. The importance of healthy eating habits cannot be overemphasized. Breaking unhealthy eating habits will actively help you overcome your anxiety (Beaton, 2016).

But if you're going to be filling yourself with unhealthy food, well, then, really you're causing the opposite to happen. On the flip side of the coin, certain forms of fasting, like intermittent fasting, can help regulate your body when it has experienced irregular sugar spikes that come from us getting a quick take-out burger when we are starving. If intermittent fasting becomes a habit, you may notice healthier outcomes and that you feel better physically. The important thing here again is the intent. When you are doing intermittent fasting, your goal is to get healthier and speed up your metabolism. When you skip breakfast because you overslept, your body is going to begin crying out for sustenance and you're either going to fill it with junk because you don't have time, or you're going to feel those low blood sugar symptoms.

While you are on your journey towards building healthier eating habits, it is also important to be mindful of the types of food that aid in reducing, and that contribute to increased anxiety. Knowing what to put into your body makes your natural response to anxiety better or worse.

BREAKING THE CYCLE

Changing the bad habits we have, or even attempting to escape from being stuck in the cycle of stress and anxiety that we're in is extremely difficult. But there are a few ways to successfully and effectively get out from being stuck where you are. The first thing you need to do is identify that you're in your stress cycle and acknowledge that it exists. You can't fight a monster that isn't real, so quit trying to hide your struggles and quit trying to tell yourself that your stress and anxiety exists. The quicker you face this part of your journey, the quicker your road to recovery begins.

Start with identifying if you are in an unhealthy stress or anxiety cycle. Do you find yourself concerned with how the day is going to pan out before it even begins? Look at yourself on a physical level. Are you exhibiting any symptoms that may allow you to believe you are facing anxiety and stress?

Once you see that you are actively in a stress and anxiety cycle, the next thing you are going to do is try to become objective in what you are facing. What I like to do is take a step back and ask myself what advice would I give to someone who is facing the exact same thing as myself at this moment. Because you're the one in your body, it's difficult to rationalize what you're going through and even harder to determine where in the stress cycle you actually are. When you step back, you can see the situation spread open in front of you, you can see your responses, and in so doing, you can determine how to jump into action and stop the cycle that you seem to be stuck in.

While you will need to handle each anxiety cycle and stress cycle on a case by case basis, being aware of where you are and what you are doing at all times, there are ways of intervening, changing your habits before time, and preventing the next big anxiety attack from happening.

Some of these "bad" habits include procrastination, phone obsessions, disorganization, and nail biting (Abramson & Seaver, 2020). These habits seem so small in the greater scheme of things but they actually hold us back a lot. Let us look at a phone obsession first. Our phones hold literally every facet of our lives on it, so the fact that it demands our attention is expected. We may find that we anxiously check our phones to make sure we don't miss out on something or we aren't left out of something. This is not healthy. And while we can't give up using our phones entirely or forever, because it is just not realistic, we can try being physically removed from our phones for specific periods of time to avoid obsessively checking it or the notifications we may receive (Abramson & Seaver, 2020).

Procrastination in itself is the epitome of the anxiety cycle. You avoid something long enough so you don't have to stress about it until it becomes unavoidable with its heaps and mounds of accompanying anxiety. One way of breaking this habit is by first acknowledging that you suffer from procrastination, that you need to get out of it, and prioritize the tasks you are avoiding by putting it at the top of your to-do list (Abramson & Seaver, 2020).

I am not asking you to jump head first into making drastic changes in your life. What I am asking you to do, and what I am guaranteeing to help you, is to start small. A few minutes a day. And if you can't manage a few minutes of change each day, why not start with 30 seconds? I guarantee you that there is nothing you could rather do in those 30 seconds, and you may end up extending those 30 seconds because you enjoy it so much!

EMBRACE THE NEW-FOUND JOURNEY

E motional regulation—this is something we try to teach kids but often we as adults don't quite grasp the concept either. When we are anxious, we have little to no emotional regulation. And the moment that we have snapped, we have yelled at our kids or our partner, or we have broken down into tears, in that moment we have no control at all.

So many times, people rush through life, and they blame work, traffic, and all the elements of life that we are expected to so tightly cling to for taking their attention away from anything that can bring a sense of calm. And while this is true for the most part, many people use this busyness as a coping mechanism to avoid the stillness, to avoid the quiet, and to actually avoid being mindful. While mindfulness is the approach that I have been taking towards anxiety and depression, many people find themselves hoping to avoid it. Perhaps the reality they are faced with is the very thing that is causing their anxiety and they rather avoid it. To those people I will say, you are stronger than your circumstances, you are stronger than your situation, and you are a conqueror. Some people can't achieve mindfulness, and that is alright. Maybe it can't benefit them now, but perhaps it can in future.

Mindfulness cannot be achieved in theory. It is a practical task. Like I mentioned before, it needs to easily fit into your life and be accommodated by what you do on a daily basis. Don't say that you are going to spend some time doing mindful meditation at 3:00 p.m. when you actually have a meeting scheduled for that time. My advice would be to make it the first thing you do. Roll out of bed and roll into a state of mindfulness.

If you are concerned that your extremely busy thoughts and your cluttered mind is going to be the very thing that stops you from being mindful, then you are not alone. Perhaps you are thinking that not even journaling or writing down your to-do list is going to help you, then might I suggest that during your mindful practices you focus on the clutter that is in your mind. Ask yourself why it seems to be so much and so heavy in your head. Confront each thought that is running wild in your head, for a brief second, give it the attention that it is demanding and ask yourself why it is there, what it needs, and what you can do to remove it from your mind. Sometimes putting it on a list is not enough to take the thought out of your mind. Sometimes, the thought needs immediate action. In that case, address it right away. But let's be honest, without confrontation through mindfulness, we might have never addressed the thoughts that are controlling our minds.

Mindfulness is not going to become your second nature immediately but it will when you make it a habit. You are going to need to remind yourself, often, to be mindful in the moment. I have been practicing mindfulness for a long time now, and yet there are times that I find myself pulling out my phone while I am with my kids at the park. But mindfulness has taught me to remind myself to be mindful. I know that sounds weird, but let me explain. I started forming the habit of mindfulness. I enjoyed it so much that I upped the dose, so to speak. I realized that I was getting more out of mindful practices than I was getting out of using my phone and so I decided to replace the one with the other—I replaced social media with mindfulness. Sometimes though, the muscle memory of the bad habit I had is still in my brain, it has not been entirely removed as yet (which I will continuously work towards), and I find myself reaching for my phone to go onto a social media app that I no longer even have. But my good habit begins ringing in my mind telling me to stop, notice what I am doing, and immediately adjust it.

It has taken me months and months, and yet I still find myself unconsciously trying to slip back into old habits. But you know what? I am patient with myself. And I acknowledge the fact that my new habit allowed me to quickly realize that the thing I was doing was not what I wanted to do. And I immediately self-corrected. And that, my friend, is a win in itself.

If simply being mindful doesn't seem like a good enough fit for you, or if you have passed and succeeded in simple mindful practices and you are looking for something more, there are formal mindful practices that you can employ. These include meditation (guided or not), yoga, and tai-chi (Living Well, n.d.).

In being patient with yourself, also remember that you may not achieve everything that mindfulness expects from you, whether it is immediately or ever, and that is perfectly fine. Let's be realistic, when you're at the park with your kids, you can't be mindful of every single stimulus that is occurring in your surroundings. Being overly stimulated may actually serve as a distractor rather than helping you ease your anxiety. Mindfulness needs to be personalized to you and to your needs. If I am with my kids, being mindful of everything may actually take my attention off my kids. Instead, I choose to be mindful with a goal, and that goal is the safety and time I am spending with my kids. So the family on the other end of the park having a picnic will not be the focus of my attention. I am going to focus on my kids, where they are, what they are doing, and who is near them. While I am not going to be preoccupied with those around us, I am going to keep an eye out for any suspicious activity or suspicious persons. Allowing myself to be mindful of too many unnecessary things means that I will lose focus on what's important and may present as an overstimulation to me. So while you are being mindful, be aware of what you're being mindful of.

THE BEAUTY OF SELF-AWARENESS

Being mindful is great, as we have already established, but let me tell you that mindfulness is nothing with self-awareness. Self-awareness is the equal yet opposite of mindfulness. While mindfulness asks you to look outwards and emotions and feelings to the external world, self-awareness prompts you to look inward, to yourself, to who you are, and how the world may respond to you. The way I like to understand self-awareness is that it is all great to smell the roses and be mindful of everything I am doing and every thought I am having, but this is useless if I am not being a good and kind person to the people around me. What good is it to take in the joy of the world when you are not actively contributing to that joy?

The nice thing about mindfulness though, is that as you venture on your mindful journey, you will find yourself more self-aware almost immediately. You will be aware not only of your feelings, but of your responses to those stimuli too.

When I talk about self-awareness, I am not talking about negative self-awareness. It's not about you feeling self-conscious, or not feeling beautiful in a particular outfit that you're wearing. This goes beyond that. While mindfulness tells you to know what you are feeling at a certain moment, self-awareness asks you why you are feeling that way. It further contributes to removing you from feeling like you're living on autopilot.

Self-awareness is based on multiple aspects, from your traits and habits, your beliefs and morals, your personal values, your psychological needs, and your physical environment. It allows you to be knowledgeable and aware of who you are and will allow you to respond to the environment in a way that is best for you. For example, being self-aware means knowing if you are an introvert or an extrovert. If you are an introvert, the idea of doing things the way an extrovert would do things will be enough to set off your anxiety. Being self-aware will allow you to engage in situations that are best suited to the person you are.

Self-awareness also allows you to better identify your triggers, it helps you know and understand what sets you off on a downward spiral and why this is the case. If you know you are someone who acts strongly to feelings of anger and frustration, and you know that certain sports games trigger those feelings, you already have some form of control over that trigger. You are now equipped with what causes feeling in you and you can either adjust your exposure to the stimulus or the response you give to the stimulus.

Our self awareness also allows us to recognize ourselves and what we hope to achieve. If we know we lack confidence and that is standing in the way of us achieving a promotion at work, then we can actively work towards dealing with this lack of confidence.

So how can you improve your self-awareness in a way that benefits your overall life and well being? Well, the first thing would be to recognize and acknowledge your emotions. Ask yourself why you are feeling a certain way, what caused it, how does this manifest emotionally, how do you react, and what are the consequences of these reactions (Magdic, 2019)?

Next, you need to pay attention to the way we talk to ourselves. Have you noticed how others always get the best and most polite versions of ourselves? But how can we be kind to others when we are not so kind to ourselves? We are often our harshest critics, and it is so easy to call ourselves a clutz when we do something wrong but assure someone else that everyone makes mistakes. We are usually the most negative with ourselves, but it's time we changed that narrative. I'm not saying you should use positive self-talk and be negative to those around you. I am saying that if you are good and kind to yourself, imagine how good and kind you can be to the world. As someone who lost many loved ones that were dear to me, I changed the narrative of my self-talk by asking if my mom and dad would be happy hearing someone else say to me what I often say to myself. The answer was that my mom and dad would have probably sent that person packing a long time ago.

Next, you need to analyze yourself. Actively note what are your strengths and weaknesses, without judging yourself. This will allow you to thrive where you are strong and work on where you are weak. And lastly, you need to reflect and be mindful—and just like that you have made a full circle from mindfulness to self-awareness and back again.

CONCLUSION

Wow, what a journey! If there is anything that you have learnt in reading this book, it is that mindfulness is the key in unlocking a peaceful and happier version of yourself. But over and above that, the power for your mindfulness to actually work lies within you.

It is so easy to underestimate ourselves, it is easy to pin the blame on ourselves, and it is easy to live with the anxiety and depression that we have gotten used to. But I am here to tell you that this is not the end game. If the version of yourself you are currently faced with is not the best version of yourself, then it is most definitely not your final version.

Some things to consider as you move through this book and begin actively employing and utilizing methods of overcoming your anxiety and depression are:

- This is not a quick and easy journey. This is not an overnight solution, but in it being a long term solution, it takes consistent work until it becomes a habit that helps you maintain your peace. It is a never ending routine and habit that you will form. It actively takes up the space that anxiety and depression once held in your life and it makes you a better version of yourself.

- Be patient with yourself. Rome wasn't built in a day, and neither were you. It took nine months for the miracle that you are to be formed. Now that you are here, it took you years to become the person you actually are. You can't undo a lifetime worth of bad habits in a day. Be patient with yourself, reign in your expectations and be understanding to your plight.

- Mindfulness is the key. While mindfulness is what I hoped to impart with you in this book, it is important to note that mindfulness looks different for everyone. The practices that I have used may not be the ones that are best for you. You may not be someone who enjoys writing down your thoughts and journaling, but nature may be your answer. Whatever it is, attempting to be mindful will set you your way to a healthier and happier version of yourself. It is a proven and tested way, not just for myself, but for others too.

- Lastly, you don't need to live with stress, anxiety, and depression, because ultimately, that is no way to live at all. You have the power to overcome, you have the ability to change your life. When someone says they are "changing their life" it doesn't mean they are making a massive change or moving to a different country. It can even mean that they are waking up five minutes earlier each morning, or that they are drinking more water. That is life changing.

Now that you are starting your journey, never for a second underestimate the power that you have. You have the power to create fear, imagine what you can do using that power to overcome the fear?

Today, I am going to remind you of something that I would like you to remind yourself of everyday hereafter: You are physically, mentally, and emotionally strong. Your anxiety and depression does not define you. You are capable of overcoming anything that you

are faced with. You are phenomenal. And most importantly, you are absolute magic.

The mere fact that you are here on this earth is a
phenomenal unfolding of events that the universe has
divulged. Now, hold your head up, and start acting like
the blessing that you are.

Here's to becoming the best version of yourself!

PLEASE LEAVE A QUICK REVIEW

Thank you for purchasing Mindful Anxiety Relief. Dealing with, acknowledging, and working through life's hard times. Some of that work comes from reading books to help us remember we have the power in ourselves if we take the time to learn and make healing a priority. It is my hope that this book will reach those who need to hear this message. Would you be interested in helping someone you may not know? If so I have an ask to make for someone you do not know. The way to get this message to those who need to start their healing journey is by reaching them. Most do judge a book by its cover and reviews. If you have found this book helpful thus far would you take a brief moment right now to leave an honest review of this book and its contents? It will cost you zero dollars and less than 1 minute. Your review will help someone out there who suffers from anxiety. It will not only help one person but everyone around them. Your review will help one more person find peace in their life. Your review will help one more person find self-love and inner peace in their life. You could be the one review that can help someone completely start transforming their life. To make this happen all you have to do is take less than 1 minute and leave a review.

GLOSSARY

- **Anxiety**: An intense feeling of dread; feeling nervous or uneasy.
- **Anxiety cycle**: The cycle of the anxiety process that often leads to chronic anxiety.
- **Chronic anxiety**: A disorder stemming from persistent anxiety that stems from sometimes irrational and constant fears.
- **Depression**: A mood disorder whereby the sufferer faces a wide variation of sadness and despair.
- **Neurons**: A granular cell tasked with the responsibility of receiving and transmitting stimuli and responses to and from the brain.
- **Neuroplasticity**: The brain's ability to "rewire" itself, to learn new things, relearn certain

functions, or adapt to certain environmental changes.

- **Stress**: Tension that is placed on the human body either physically, mentally, emotionally, or hormonally.
- **Stress cycles**: The cycle that the body goes through in processing stress and stressful situations, from the input of a stimulus, the psychological release of hormones, the internal response to the stimulus, and the dissipation.

REFERENCES

Abramson, S., & Seaver, M. (2020). *How to Break 11 Common Bad Habits for Good*. Real Simple. https://www.realsimple.com/work-life/life-strategies/how-to-break-bad-habits#dbe8b231-0486-4e6d-b827-f7953ae6cad0

Banks, D. (2016, April 4). *What is brain plasticity and why is it so important?* The Conversation. https://theconversation.com/what-is-brain-plasticity-and-why-is-it-so-important-55967

Beaton, C. (2016). *8 Habits That Make Millennials Stressed, Anxious And Unproductive.* Forbes. https://www.forbes.com/sites/carolinebeaton/2016/02/18/8-habits-that-make-millennials-stressed-anxious-and-unproductive/?sh=53ee2dd01ef1

Benisek, A. (2020). *Depression and Anxiety: Are They Hereditary?* WebMD. https://www.webmd.com/depression/are-depression-anxiety-hereditary#:~:text=lower%20your%20risk.-

Brown, J., & Wong, J. (2017, June 6). *How Gratitude Changes You and Your Brain.* Greater Good. https://greatergood.berkeley.edu/article/item/how_gratitude_changes_you_and_your_brain

Cherry, K. (2020, April 21). *The Importance of Maintaining Structure and Routine During Stressful Times.* Verywell Mind. https://www.verywellmind.com/the-importance-of-keeping-a-routine-during-stressful-times-4802638

Clear, J. (2014, March 27). *I'm Using These 3 Simple Steps to Actually Stick with Good Habits.* James Clear. https://jamesclear.com/small-habits

Cleveland Clinic. (2020). *Hemispherectomy: What Is It, Definition & Recovery.* Cleveland Clinic. https://my.clevelandclinic.org/health/treatments/17092-hemispherectomy#:~:text=What%20is%20a%20hemispherectomy%3F

Cleveland Clinic. (2022). *What are Adaptogens & Types.* Cleveland Clinic. https://my.clevelandclinic.org/health/drugs/22361-adaptogens#:~:text=Adaptogens%20are%20plants%20and%20mushrooms

Embrace Sexual Wellness. (2020). *Stress Cycles: What they Are and How to Break Them — Embrace Sexual Wellness.* Embrace Sexual Wellness. https://www.embracesexualwellness.com/esw-blog/stresscycles

Ferber, S. (2020). *How the 90-second rule can change your life | The Daniel Island News.* Thedanielislandnews.com. http://thedanielisland-news.com/opinions/how-90-second-rule-can-change-your-life#:~:text=%E2%80%9CFeelings%20are%20like%20ocean%20waves

Fishbane, M. D. (2015, September 30). *Change Is a Choice: Nurturing Neuroplasticity in Your Life.* GoodTherapy.org Therapy Blog. https://www.goodtherapy.org/blog/change-is-a-choice-nurturing-neuroplasticity-in-your-life-0930154#:~:text=Neuroplastici-ty%20in%20Adulthood

Frothingham, S. (2019, May 24). *Caffeine and anxiety: How does your caffeine habit affect anxiety?* Healthline. https://www.healthline.com/health/caffeine-and-anxiety#caffeine-and-anxiety

Good Reads. (n.d.). *A quote by Brian Tracy.* Www.goodreads.com. Retrieved August 18, 2022, from https://www.goodreads.com/quotes/23018-you-cannot-control-what-happens-to-you-but-you-can

Grohol, J. M. (2016, May 17). *Changing Our Routines and Habits.* Psych Central. https://psychcentral.com/lib/changing-our-routines-and-habits#1

Harvard Health Publishing. (2020, July 6). *Understanding the Stress Response. Harvard Health;* Harvard Health. https://www.health.harvard.edu/staying-healthy/understanding-the-stress-response

Hims Editorial Team. (2021). *Anxiety Triggers: How to Identify & Overcome Them.* Hims. https://www.forhims.com/blog/common-anxiety-triggers

Holly J. (2022). *Medline Reviews - Investigative Medical Journalism.* Www.medline-Reviews.com. https://www.medline-reviews.com/how-ashwa-helped-my-anxiety-us/

Khouja, J. N., Munafò, M. R., Tilling, K., Wiles, N. J., Joinson, C., Etchells, P. J., John, A., Hayes, F. M., Gage, S. H., & Cornish, R. P. (2019). Is screen time associated with anxiety or depression in young people? Results from a UK birth cohort. *BMC Public Health*, 19(1). https://doi.org/10.1186/s12889-018-6321-9

Life Couseling Institute. (2021, June 15). *10 Daily Habits That Can Reduce Your Anxiety - Willowbrook - Park Ridge*. Life Counseling Institute. https://lifecounselinginstitute.com/10-daily-habits-that-can-reduce-your-anxiety/

Living Well. (n.d.). *Being aware of yourself and the world | Mindfulness for mental wellbeing*. Living Well. https://livingwell.org.au/well-being/five-ways-to-mental-wellbeing/be-aware-of-yourself-and-the-world/

Magdic, J. (2019, July 28). *5 WAYS TO IMPROVE YOUR SELF-AWARENESS AND LIVE A BETTER LIFE*. WellSeek. https://wellseek.co/2019/07/28/5-ways-to-improve-your-self-awareness-and-live-a-better-life/

Mandriota, M. (2022, March 9). *Understanding the Cycle of Anxiety and How to Cope*. Psych Central. https://psychcentral.com/anxiety/cycle-of-anxiety#signs

Mateos-Aparicio, P., & Rodríguez-Moreno, A. (2019). The Impact of Studying Brain Plasticity. *Frontiers in Cellular Neuroscience, 13*(66). https://doi.org/10.3389/fncel.2019.00066

Mayo Clinic Staff. (2018). *Anxiety disorders - Symptoms and causes*. Mayo Clinic. https://www.mayoclinic.org/diseases-conditions/anxiety/symptoms-causes/syc-20350961#:~:text=Feeling%20nervous%2C%20restless%20or%20tense

Mcquaid, M. (2014). *5 Ways to Turn Tiny Habits into Big Changes | Live Happy*. Live Happy. https://www.livehappy.com/self/5-ways-to-turn-tiny-habits-into-big-changes

MedlinePlus. (2020, September 17). *Is intelligence determined by genetics?: MedlinePlus genetics*. Medlineplus.gov. https://medlineplus.gov/genetics/understanding/traits/intelligence/

Milkman, K. (2021). *How to build a habit in 5 steps, according to science*. CNN. https://edition.cnn.com/2021/11/29/health/5-steps-habit-builder-wellness/index.html

Mind. (2021, February). *Anxiety signs and symptoms*. Www.mind.org.uk.

https://www.mind.org.uk/information-support/types-of-mental-health-problems/anxiety-and-panic-attacks/symptoms/

Moncrieff, J., Cooper, R. E., Stockmann, T., Amendola, S., Hengartner, M. P., & Horowitz, M. A. (2022). The serotonin theory of depression: a systematic umbrella review of the evidence. *Molecular Psychiatry*, 1–14. https://doi.org/10.1038/s41380-022-01661-0

Nall, R. (2022, May 23). *Your Guide to Brain Plasticity*. Healthline; Healthline Media. https://www.healthline.com/health/brain-plasticity-and-behavior

NEA Member Benefits. (n.d.). *5 Healthy Habits to Get Through Tough Times*. Www.neamb.com. Retrieved August 27, 2022, from https://www.neamb.com/family-and-wellness/how-to-create-healthy-habits-a-step-at-a-time

Peterson, T. J. (2022). *Mindfulness for Anxiety: What It Is, How It Works, & Effectiveness*. Choosing Therapy. https://www.choosingtherapy.com/mindfulness-for-anxiety/

Repich, D. (n.d.). *Six Simple Habits That Defeat Anxiety*. Mental Health Association San Francisco. https://www.mentalhealthsf.org/six-simple-habits-that-defeat-anxiety/

Ries, S. K., Dronkers, N. F., & Knight, R. T. (2016). Choosing words: left hemisphere, right hemisphere, or both? Perspective on the lateralization of word retrieval. *Annals of the New York Academy of Sciences*, 1369(1), 111–131. https://doi.org/10.1111/nyas.12993

Schnatz, R. (2021, March 23). *Why Women Worry: How Hormones Affect Anxiety and What We Can Do About It*. Virginia Physicians for Women. https://vpfw.com/blog/why-women-worry-how-hormones-affect-anxiety-and-what-we-can-do-about-it/#:~:text=Your%20body%20produces%20stress%20hormones

Star, K. (2020). *Are There Potential Benefits to Having Anxiety?* Verywell Mind. https://www.verywellmind.com/benefits-of-anxiety-2584134#:~:text=Even%20though%20it%20may%20seem

Start Tiny. (n.d.). *Tiny Habits*. https://tinyhabits.com/start-tiny/

Suttie, J. (2019, October 28). *The Mindfulness Skill That Is Crucial for Stress*. Greater Good. https://greatergood.berkeley.edu/article/item/the_mindfulness_skill_that_is_crucial_for_stress

TEDx. (2016). *Emotional Mastery: The Gifted Wisdom of Unpleasant Feelings | Dr Joan Rosenberg | TEDxSantaBarbara* [VIDEO]. In www.youtube.com. https://www.youtube.com/watch?v=EKy19WzkPxE&ab_channel=TEDxTalks

TEDx. (2013). *Hardwiring happiness: Dr. Rick Hanson at TEDxMarin 2013* [VIDEO]. In www.youtube.com. https://www.youtube.com/watch?v=jpuDyGgIeh0&ab_channel=TEDxTalks

TEDx. (2017a). *How to cope with anxiety | Olivia Remes | TEDxUHasselt* [VIDEO]. In www.youtube.com. https://www.youtube.com/watch?v=WWloIAQpMcQ&ab_channel=TEDxTalks

TEDx. (2017b). *How to end stress, unhappiness and anxiety to live in a beautiful state | Preetha ji | TEDxKC* [VIDEO]. In www.youtube.com. https://www.youtube.com/watch?v=TqxxCYnAxo8&t=29s&ab_channel=TEDxTalks

TEDx. (2015). *The Secret of Becoming Mentally Strong | Amy Morin | TEDxOcala* [VIDEO]. Www.youtube.com. https://www.youtube.com/watch?v=TFbv757kup4&ab_channel=TEDxTalks

The Recovery Villiage. (2022). *Identifying & Coping with Anxiety Triggers | The Recovery Village.* The Recovery Village Drug and Alcohol Rehab. https://www.therecoveryvillage.com/mental-health/anxiety/anxiety-triggers/

Therapist Aid. (2018). *What is the Cycle of Anxiety?* Www.youtube.com. https://www.youtube.com/watch?v=-CAd9o9OlqM&ab_channel=TherapistAid

Therapy in a Nutshell. (2019). *Rewiring the Anxious Brain: Neuroplasticity and the Anxiety Cycle: Anxiety Skills #21* [VIDEO]. Www.youtube.com. https://www.youtube.com/watch?v=zTuX_ShUrw0&ab_channel=TherapyinaNutshell

Walesh, S. G. (n.d.). *Using the Power of Habits to Work Smarter.* Www.helpingyouengineeryourfuture.com. http://www.helpingyouengineeryourfuture.com/habits-work-smarter.htm

Williams, S. C. P. (2014). *Genes don't just influence your IQ—they determine how well you do in school.* Www.science.org. https://www.science.org/content/article/genes-dont-just-influence-your-iq-they-determine-how-well-you-do-school#:~:text=Researchers%20have%20previously%20shown%20that

Young, K. (2016, May 18). *Overcoming Anxiety: The Remarkable (and Proven) Power of Mindfulness - How, Why, What.* Hey Sigmund. https://www.heysigmund.com/overcoming-anxiety-mindfulness/

Printed in Great Britain
by Amazon

23346647R00088